DATE DUE

APR 1 8 2001	

Before
the
Heroes
Came

T. H. Baughman

BEFORE THE HEROES CAME

Antarctica in the 1890s

University of Nebraska Press

Lincoln and London

Copyright © 1994 by the
University of Nebraska Press
All rights reserved
Manufactured in the United
States of America

The paper in this book
meets the minimum
requirements of American
National Standard
for Information Sciences –
Permanence of
Paper for Printed Library
Materials,
ANSI Z39.48–1984.
Library of Congress
Cataloging-in-Publication Data
Baughman, T. H., 1947–
Before the heroes came :
Antarctica in the 1890s /
T. H. Baughman.
p. cm.
Includes bibliographical
references and index.
ISBN 0-8032-1228-3
(alk. paper)
1. Antarctic
regions—Discovery and
exploration—History.
I. Title. G870.B26   1993
919.8'9—dc20
93-1056   CIP

To Verna M. Baughman
and Richard L. Greaves

Contents

ILLUSTRATIONS

Photographs

Maps

Preface

South of the sixtieth parallel lies the Antarctic continent. Comprising ten percent of the earth's surface and more than forty percent of the world's supply of fresh water, it remained in cold isolation for centuries. Ice abounds: were ten percent of the mass to break off in a single day, the level of the world's oceans would rise and flood many coastal cities worldwide. The Ross Ice Shelf is situated in a bay larger than France, and icebergs bigger than Rhode Island have calved and floated northward.[1] Yet only as humans interact with Antarctica does the area become of interest to the historian. Since the International Geophysical Year (1956–58) the world has paid the southern regions increasing attention as awareness of natural resources and of the possibilities for economic exploitation has grown. As the largest landmass governed by international agreement, Antarctica is an experiment in the peaceful cooperation of nations. Thus the lack of attention paid to it by social scientists is curious.

Historians have concentrated on the Heroic Era, 1901–22, from the launch of the *Discovery* expedition[2] to the death of Sir Ernest Shackleton. The voyages of these two decades were filled with fascinating adventures. The story of Robert Falcon Scott's last expedition and the saga of Shackleton's *Endurance* have thrilled readers for three-quarters of a century. In concentrating on these activities, however, writers have slighted the men of the 1890s, the forerunners of the later adventurers. Decisions made in that decade had a profound effect on the progress of science in Antarctica for more than two generations.

This study surveys the events that led to a renewal of interest in the Antarctic in the late nineteenth century and explains how these actions shaped later exploration. After a brief review of events before 1885, the story notes why and how various groups attempted to launch ventures. The whaling voyages of middecade are described along with the unsuccessful attempts by individuals to launch scientific endeavors. The voyage of the *Southern Cross*, the pivotal journey of the period, is discussed in detail. Finally, the achievements of these pioneers are assessed.

Three people are preeminent in this account. Carsten E. Borchgrevink, the brusque Anglo-Norwegian who was the first person to set foot on the last continent, played a crucial role by commanding the pioneering *Southern Cross* expedition. This voyage accomplished valuable research, although its work was ignored by contemporaries and has been overlooked by subsequent historians. The second figure was Sir Clements R. Markham, president of the Royal Geographical Society, a single-minded man driven to launch a British expedition in the image of the Arctic ventures of his youth. Markham denigrated Borchgrevink's efforts and ignored the Norwegian's achievements. A Scot, William S. Bruce, was the third adventurer. Having sailed with the Dundee whaling expedition, he returned, like Borchgrevink, determined to lead his own endeavor. Unlike Borchgrevink, who feigned scientific interest but sought adventure, Bruce was a scientist and explorer, of the same type that directed the national expeditions launched by Sweden and Germany in the first years of the twentieth century. Britain did not follow the example of the continental countries but chose instead a naval officer, Robert Falcon Scott, who led the *Discovery* expedition (1901–4). By this action the pattern of British Antarctic exploration was established: science was made the handmaiden of adventure.

However appealing the adventures of the Heroic Era, the men of the 1890s faced similar dangers in attempting to lift the veil of the unknown from the "land of unsurpassed desolation."[3] The men of the last decade of the Victorian era made influential initial efforts to open the continent for science before the heroes came.

Many people contributed to the completion of this work. I am grateful to Richard L. Greaves, Alexander Bassin, Delores Bryant, Celine Carrigan,

Paul G. Halpern, Karen Melton, and Ralph V. Turner for reading drafts of this account.

Among those who assisted in my research in England are Christine Kelly, archivist of the Royal Geographical Society, and Robert Headland, archivist of the Scott Polar Research Institute, whom I thank for their kindness and endless patience. David Wileman and Jayne Dunlop, librarians of the RGS, were extremely helpful and made me feel that the RGS library is my home in London. In the United States I was provided useful information and guidance by Chris Renz of the National Geographic Society and Douglas R. McManis of the American Geographical Society. Janet Vetter provided information about her father, Frederick Cook. Oddvar Vasstveit, librarian at the Universitetsbiblioteket in Oslo graciously assisted me with materials held in his archives. Peter Speak provided me with insight into the career of William S. Bruce.

I wish to thank Ian M. Whillans, world-renowned glaciologist, for taking me South as his token humanist. From my publishing days I want to note the friendship of James Dewberry and Jack Edmonds. Jim helped keep me sane during various tough moments. The highest tribute I can pay to Jack is that he is a Marine who grew up.

Two friends whom I rely on for advice over a wide range of subjects are Russell P. Buchan and Paul Davidson. My friendship with Russell dates from our undergraduate days at Stetson University, and I count our quarter-century friendship as one of the treasures of my life. More than anyone else, Paul kept me in publishing, encouraging me to pursue both a career and my dreams.

From my days teaching at a small women's college in Georgia I want to acknowledge the support and encouragement of Ronald Bird and Robert Khoury and the inspiration I gained from Mark Ledbetter.

No one suffered more on a day-to-day basis from the process of producing this work than Karen Melton. I appreciate her kindness and support more than I can say.

The dedication serves notice of my gratitude for two people who have been extremely important to me and who have sustained and nurtured me. The credit for any pleasure you receive from reading this story should be given to them.

Finally, I want to thank Michael and Julie McBride for their comradeship and the hundreds of sublimely pleasant hours I have passed in their company, both in this country and abroad.

ONE

The White Enigma

The ancient Greeks, apparently moved by the same sense of proportion that created the gracious lines of the Parthenon, hypothesized that a landmass like Antarctica must exist, for they projected that a southern continent must balance the lands of the Northern Hemisphere. Around 530 B.C. Pythagoras postulated that the earth was round because the sphere was the form closest to perfection. His theory was reinforced by the travels of two explorers, Hanno, who in the fifth century B.C. sailed as far south as Sierra Leone, and Pytheas, who around 320 B.C. traveled as far as the Arctic ice pack, crossing the Arctic Circle. From the spherical conception of earth came the very name *Antarctic:* the northern constellation Arctos (the Bear) gave its name to the northernmost regions; balance required a corresponding region opposite the Arctic, the Antarctic.[1] Thus the Greeks supposed that a southern landmass existed but never actually observed it. They assumed that the world was divided into five zones, one of which was so extremely hot at the equator that life within it was impossible. Beyond this impassable zone was another temperate zone and below that a second frozen area, mirroring the one in the north.[2] This southern frozen land was noted on Ptolemy's map as a terra incognita, an idea that became fixed in the minds of geographers. In part the history of Antarctica is the gradual elimination of the word *incognita* from the maps of the region.[3]

Medieval geographers had difficulty explaining how people could exist on the opposite side of the globe outside the pale of the church's teaching. While some, such as the Venerable Bede, kept alive the concept of a spherical world, most regarded the earth as flat, an idea for which many found evidence in Scripture. H. R. Mill, a noted early twentieth-century historian of the Antarctic, has cogently argued that medieval scholars hesitated to describe an Antarctic region because it was heresy to hypothesize people outside the biblical description of the known world. Clerical authorities rejected empirical evidence of contemporary travelers which was counter to church teaching.[4]

Western geographical knowledge expanded with the discovery of the route to the East. Voyages sponsored by Portugal's Prince Henry the Navigator (1394–1460) not only found an alternate route to the riches of Asia but helped limit the possible area of Ptolemy's terra incognita. From the time of Prince Henry's drive southward, adventurers pushed south along the African coast in the desire to reach India, an effort that also took them toward the pole. These attempts to extend the southernmost point reached by humans, which continued until the successes of Roald Amundsen and Robert Falcon Scott in 1911 and 1912, provide a recurrent theme in an investigation of the exploration of the southern regions.[5]

The recovery of the ideas of the ancients and the recognition that southern regions might exist prompted an effort to determine the possible location of Antarctica. Although Phoenician sailors almost certainly circumnavigated Africa in the eighth century B.C., the established southernmost point of exploration by Europeans was Cape Nun (28° 46′ N), passed by Gil Eannes in 1433 or 1434.[6] Prince Henry's successors continued until they proved that Africa could be rounded. Coincidentally, by doing so they demonstrated that any southern landmass was not connected to Africa.

The sixteenth and seventeenth centuries saw a gradual reduction of the number of possible locations for a southern continent. Maps of the period showed a huge Antarctic continent covering a vast unexplored area of the globe. In the sixteenth century the remarkable accounts of Amerigo Vespucci of Italy and Sieur Paulmyer de Gonneville of France mentioned the sighting of southern lands. The discovery by Spain's Ferdinand Magellan of the strait that bears his name suggested that the land to the south of it could be the northernmost part of the fabled southern continent. His circumnavigation was followed by that of Sir Francis Drake (c. 1540/43–

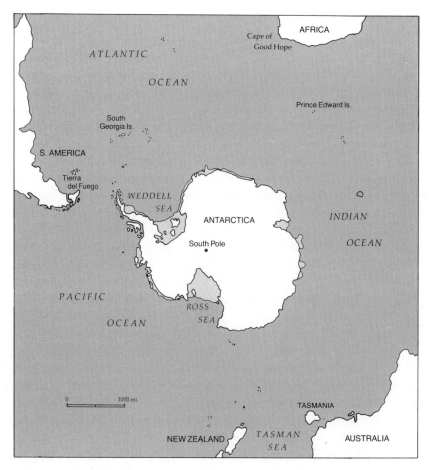

Map 1
Antarctica in Context

1596), who was instructed by the government of Elizabeth I to investigate the existence of "Terra Australis Incognita." He reached his furthest south at approximately 57° S after being blown off course in the direction of Antarctica. In 1578 Drake proved that Tierra del Fuego was an island and not part of any continental landmass.[7]

Seeing himself as a new Columbus, Pedro Fernandez de Quiros of Portugal set sail in 1605 to uncover the riches of the South. Driven by storms, he discovered the New Hebrides, which he mistakenly thought were the edge of a new continent. Instead of pushing further south, he remained there for a month before returning to Peru. His second in command,

Juan Torres, circumnavigated New Guinea, removing the possibility that another outcropping of the southern continent existed in this latitude. In 1642 a Dutchman, Abel Tasman (1603–59), sailed around Australia, disproving the theory of early discoverers that it was part of Antarctica.

Up to this point pushing back the frontiers of the South had been the work of adventurers, but at the end of the seventeenth century the first scientific expedition was sent to Antarctic waters. Then, as in the nineteenth century, the need to study the earth's magnetic field was a motivation. Edmund Halley (1656–1742), the English astronomer royal, commanded HMS *The Pink* (1698–1700) to conduct magnetic observations. It was the first purely scientific expedition by sea under any flag. Halley was in command of the ship as well as the overall director of the expedition (difficulties that arose from civilian command of a naval vessel prevented a repetition of the experiment at the time of Captain James Cook's journey). Halley proceeded as far as 52° S, where he encountered ice. Unprepared for the damage such conditions can inflict, he retreated northward. This voyage resulted in the first map of magnetic variation for the South Atlantic and Pacific and a new method of determining longitude by observing osculations of the fixed stars.[8] The immediate and practical results of this first scientific foray to the southern regions were charts that made sailing in these waters safer by allowing a more accurate determination of longitude.

Four eighteenth-century expeditions helped to fix the location of the continent. Jean-Baptiste Charles Bouvet de Lozier (1705–86) set out in 1738 to discover Antarctica. Pushing through the South Atlantic until he reached the edge of the ice pack, the French explorer proved that no continent existed as far as 54° 40' S. He sailed for several hundred miles along a latitude of roughly 55° S. Bouvet de Lozier was the first to describe in detail the Antarctic tabular icebergs, named for their flat tops. He sighted penguins and seals, which he assumed indicated nearby land. Noting that since icebergs were found at the southern latitude that corresponds to the northern latitude where Belfast is situated, he surmised that any new continent would be covered with ice. He discovered an island (54° 26' S, 3° 24' E) that he called Cape Circumcision, known today by the name of its discoverer. So isolated is this place that it was unseen again until the 1898 German expedition, which fixed its location with greater accuracy than had Bouvet de Lozier.[9]

A second Frenchman, Marion-Dufresne, embarked in 1772 with in-

structions from Louis XVI to visit the southern continent and New Zealand while returning a Tahitian native who had been visiting France.
Marion-Dufresne discovered the Marion and Crozet Islands (roughly
47° S), which he incorrectly believed would be on the edge of the continent. He called them Terre d'Espérance.

A third Frenchman, Yves Joseph de Kerguelen-Tremarec, set out in
1771 in the hope of finding a southern continent in a temperate zone. He
sailed from Mauritius southward on a mission to establish commercial
relations with the natives of a southern land, a new region that, it was
hoped, would provide some compensation for the recent loss of Canada.
Sighting an island at 49° 40' S which he called New France, he concluded
that it was a land rich in natural resources and having great promise for
commercial exploitation, but bad weather and fog prevented him from
landing and verifying his thesis. Back in France, he hailed the potential
wealth of the area and then returned the following year to continue his
explorations. His second visit to New France proved how desolate and
inhospitable the land was. Disillusioned, he changed the name to Land
of Desolation. Known today as Iles Kerguelen, it is distinguished largely
for the peculiar type of cabbage that grows there.

Speculation dating back to the Greeks that a large temperate southern continent existed was ended definitively by the voyages (1768–80) of
Captain James Cook (1728–79). Even late in the eighteenth century, serious geographers such as Alexander Dalrymple (1737–1808) had continued
to argue that a large, habitable, continental landmass existed. Dalrymple
hoped to lead an expedition to prove his theory, but even though he was
a candidate of the Royal Society, the problems experienced with Edmund
Halley's civilian command of a warship precluded Dalrymple's leading
what we now know as the Cook expedition. Sent to the South Seas to
study the transit of Venus and secretly instructed to look for new land to
be exploited for Britain's gain, Captain Cook began the long association
of the British navy with Antarctic exploration. By circumnavigating the
world at a higher latitude than had previously been reached, he proved
that any southern continent must lie far south of the temperate zone. He
also surmised that land existed to the south because the icebergs were
made of fresh, not salt, water. He asserted that the sighting of two species
of birds that required land for nesting indicated that ground would be
found south of the ice.[10]

Cook's achievements were made possible by several technological advances. The newly developed chronometer enabled the expedition to be the first to have a good idea of longitude as well as latitude. The chronometer is a timepiece that maintains accuracy despite the movements of the ship and the strain of winding the instrument. To figure longitude it was essential to have a means of exact time-keeping. Developing this instrument was so important to the world's leading naval power that in 1714 the British government offered a prize of twenty thousand pounds, won by John Harrison, for the first successful chronometer. Similar improvements were made in the sextant, a mirrored instrument that indicates latitude.[11]

On 17 January 1773 Cook was the first to cross the Antarctic Circle. Karl Fricker, turn-of-the-century German historian, believed Cook's voyage to be the beginning of the modern era of Antarctic exploration. During the second year's voyage, on 30 January 1774, Cook reached the furthest south of the cruise (71° 10' S, 106° 54' W) but was blocked from proceeding beyond this point by ice. Each winter the water surrounding the Antarctic continent freezes to a distance as much as eleven hundred miles from the mainland. Altogether this ice can contain an area roughly three times the size of the United States, or eleven million square miles. As the summer approaches, this ice warms, breaks up, and is driven northward by currents and winds. It forms a gauntlet that ships must navigate en route south. Cook's ships were not equipped for work in the ice.[12]

Halted less than one day's sail from the coast of Antarctica, Cook surmised that the ice he encountered extended to the pole. He discovered South Georgia Island, topologically similar to Antarctic land.[13] Regarding the southern lands that he had failed to see, he commented: "Should anyone possess the resolution and the fortitude to elucidate this point by pushing yet further south than I have done, I shall not envy him the fame of his discovery, but I make bold that the world will derive no benefit from it."[14] Cook's voyages were a watershed in Antarctic exploration. No longer could there be hope of finding an Antarctic continent in a temperate climate. Without the possibilities of native or trade exploitation, interest in further exploration waned.

Commerce was the motivation for the next round of Antarctic activity. Demand for furs and animal oils exceeded the declining production from the Arctic, and sealers embarked for South Georgia Island in search of the species Cook had reported. They quickly discovered, exploited, and depleted the seal population of the region.[15] In the early nineteenth century,

American sealers were the leading figures in Antarctic waters. Sealers extracted oil and sold the skins in China for substantial gains. Because secrecy was the key to preserving profits, the extent of exploration in the first two decades of the nineteenth century is largely unknown.

It is curious that the Antarctic continent should lie unseen for centuries and then be "discovered" almost simultaneously by explorers from three different nations. The controversy surrounding the discovery of the continent does not concern us here beyond noting that in 1820 and 1821 Captain Nathaniel Palmer of Connecticut, Captain Edward Bransfield of England, and Admiral Fabian Gottlieb von Bellingshausen of Russia all sighted Antarctica.[16] Palmer was searching for whales or seals; Bransfield was investigating possible naval base locations; Bellingshausen was directed by Alexander I to explore as part of the czar's program to expand his realm. All sighted Antarctic lands within weeks of one another. Palmer and Bellingshausen even sighted each other, and Palmer visited the admiral aboard his flagship.[17]

After Antarctica's discovery, three factors contributed to the renewal of interest in the continent in the early nineteenth century. The sightings of Palmer, Bransfield, and Bellingshausen opened a brief period of exploration motivated by commercial concerns. In addition, geography became a popular field, and the geographical societies founded in the major capitals of Europe stimulated curiosity about the polar regions.[18] Finally, growing scientific disciplines such as magnetism, meteorology, and oceanography needed information obtainable only from polar research.

In the 1830s several sealers explored Antarctic waters in search of whales and seals. In 1823 James Weddell (1787–34), with a crew of thirty-five in the *Jane* and the *Beaufoy*, sailed into what we now know as the Weddell Sea; he found it unusually free of ice. Combining sealing and exploration, he pushed southward until conditions dictated a retreat, establishing, on 20 February 1823, a new furthest south at 74° 15′ S and 34° 16′ 45″, 214 nautical miles further than Cook's mark. Safety for his crew prompted him to return home, which he reached in 1824 after sealing in Tierra del Fuego.[19] The Enderby brothers, who directed a Scottish sealing firm, were particularly successful in linking exploration and commercial activity and instructed their captains to be alert to the possibilities of geographical discovery and to make simple meteorological observations. Captain John Biscoe, sailing for the Enderbys, made several attempts to find land beyond the Antarctic Circle but each time was stopped by ice. In 1838 and 1839 John Balleny discovered a five-island chain that he named for himself (66° 44' S, 163° 11' E). In doing so he demonstrated that the ice barrier surrounding the continent might not be impenetrable.[20]

American sealers were active in these waters in the 1830s and 1840s, whereas British interest declined. Although abortive efforts were made to establish a whaling or sealing industry based in Australia, by the late 1830s the population of seals had been largely depleted, and sealers abandoned their efforts in the South for the next forty years.

In the meantime, events in the Arctic had some bearing on developments in the Antarctic. In 1827 Captain William E. Parry attempted to reach the North Magnetic Pole, attaining a latitude of 82° 45' N. Four years later, on 1 June 1831, James Clark Ross (1800–62) reached the North Magnetic Pole.[21]

Interest in the South was further stimulated by the several geographical societies that sent expeditions to various unexplored parts of the world, including the polar regions. At the same time, scientists showed increasing interest in the earth's magnetic field, which had been described by the German scientist Carl Friedrich Gauss (1777–1855). Gauss had estimated the location of the South Magnetic Pole, but confirmation of his theories required investigation in polar regions. Ross's exploration of the Arctic created a demand for similar geographical discoveries in the Antarctic.

Three scientific expeditions set forth in the late 1830s and early 1840s. The French sent Jules-Sébastien-César Dumont d'Urville (1790–1842), a veteran of charting expeditions in the Mediterranean, where, as a sidelight to his work, he helped the French government acquire the Venus de Milo. He also had experience in the South Pacific, where he collected many new species of flora and fauna. In September 1837 he sailed from Toulon to the Antarctic, exploring more than three hundred miles of coastline and adding greatly to science's knowledge of Antarctica. He named the Adélie penguin for his wife. Concurrently, at the direction of the United States government, Lieutenant Charles Wilkes commanded a badly equipped, ill-fated expedition. Following on the heels of these two voyages was that of Britain's James Clark Ross, inspired by the efforts of the Royal Society and the British Association for the Advancement of Science.

Ross, in the *Erebus* and the *Terror*, avoided the path of the French and American expeditions and made a remarkable voyage in the years 1840–

8

43. He proved that the ice pack could be navigated and that beyond it were open waters. He discovered a body of water, now known as the Ross Sea, and sailed far enough south to discover the two volcanoes he named for his ships. He called the place he saw to the west South Victoria Land after Queen Victoria and explored more than five hundred miles of the Antarctic shore. Ross sighted the great ice shelf, the most astounding of the physical features of the area, and gave it the name it had throughout the Heroic Era: the Great Ice Barrier. Now known as the Ross Ice Shelf, it dazzled the imagination of Antarctic explorers and followers of southern expeditions. A sheer cliff one hundred and fifty feet high, it formed an absolute barrier for ships. Affording no shore, it seemed to guard the Antarctic from further exploration unless one could somehow land and travel across it. Beyond the Great Ice Barrier might lie land or, as Ross thought, more water, an extension of the great polar sea. Ross's mark of 78° 10' stood as the southernmost point achieved by an explorer until Carsten E. Borchgrevink surpassed it in 1900.[22]

No further Antarctic exploration followed Ross's expedition for a period of forty years. Ross had shown that a great landmass existed south of the Antarctic Circle, but it was not yet known if it was a series of islands or a continent.

After Ross the Antarctic largely faded from the public's mind, partly because attention was focused on the Arctic during this period. The Franklin expeditions captured the popular imagination, especially in England.[23] The Arctic, with its proximity to northern Europe and with a native population, remained the center of interest. Improved methods of hunting whales enabled the industry to subsist in the fifties and sixties, avoiding the doldrums that would characterize it in the 1880s. Finally, once geographers satisfied themselves that Antarctica was not a fit locale for colonization, the continent attracted little attention until sufficient scientific interest crystallized.[24]

As new questions were raised in the areas of magnetism, oceanography, meteorology, and navigation, the Antarctic became the place to find many of the answers. Though no one ventured into Antarctic waters in the period, the quest for knowledge about the South Polar regions was kept alive by several determined individuals, notably Matthew F. Maury (1806–73) and Georg Balthasar von Neumayer (1826–1909). Maury, an American naval officer who became the superintendent of the U.S. Hydrographic Office, was a pioneer in hydrography and oceanography and was

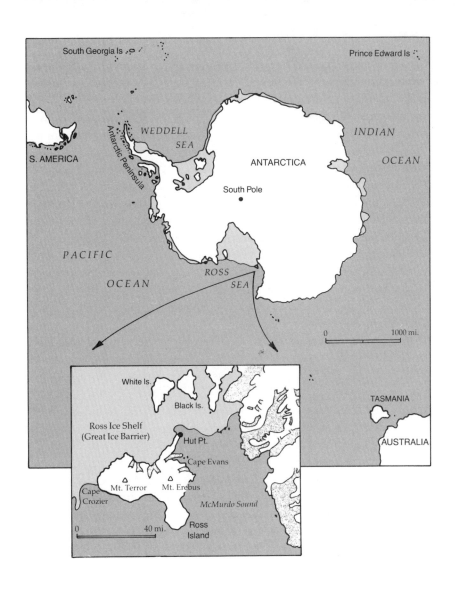

Map 2
Antarctica

interested in Antarctica not only for scientific reasons but for the practical impact such knowledge had on navigation, sailing, and commerce.
In the days before steamships dominated international commerce, vessels
found that sailing further south of the Cape of Good Hope brought more
favorable winds. Unfortunately, those routes were threatened by icebergs.
More information was needed about currents, ice conditions, and the impact of Antarctic regions on weather. In Brussels in 1853 Maury organized
an international marine conference that established criteria to standardize
record keeping for air and sea movements during voyages. To gain additional data Maury wanted a scientific expedition sent to Antarctic waters.
His efforts to persuade the American government to launch such an expedition ended in 1861 when the Civil War eliminated all possibility that
the United States would devote resources to such an endeavor.[25]

Von Neumayer had been influenced by the ideas of Maury and was
keenly interested in oceanography and hydrography. After his university
days he pursued his scientific interests in Australia, where he spent his
time roughing it in the outback and developing plans for an expedition to
the Antarctic. Returning to Germany, he enlisted the assistance of Alexander von Humboldt (1769–1859), a leading authority on earth sciences,
especially terrestrial magnetism; he had previously been interested in
the Antarctic. The two persuaded Maximilian II of Bavaria to donate two
thousand pounds to establish a magnetic observatory in Australia.

In Melbourne, von Neumayer founded his observatory and eventually
got the local government to assist him financially. By 1864 he had finished his magnetic survey and prepared to return to Germany, leaving
a successful record of scientific achievement and a versatile guide to ice
conditions for navigators approaching Australia. Once in Germany he
persuaded the Vienna Academy of Sciences to outfit an expedition to
study the transit of Venus in 1874. That research, he hoped, would solve
the question of the earth's distance from the sun, but it required at least
one observer as far south as possible—ideally, below the Antarctic Circle.
Financial backing was offered, but the plan did not come to fruition because of the outbreak of war in Europe in 1870.[26]

By this point it had been established that land existed south of the Antarctic Circle, although whether it was a continent or a series of islands was
uncertain. It was also known that some value existed in learning about
it, but nothing had been done since Ross's return in 1843. During this
time the commercial side of Antarctic knowledge was being developed

as the British Admiralty began to issue ice charts of southern waters and von Neumayer published his *Register of Voyages*, which supplied related information.

At the urging of the Royal Society, the British government sent a ship to survey the oceans in the Antarctic regions. Departing in 1872, the *Challenger* performed great service, extending the knowledge of oceans, currents, and navigation. Investigations conducted during the voyage disproved, for example, the theory that no life existed in deep water. Deep-water dredging greatly expanded the understanding of deep-water flora and fauna.[27]

What the explorers before the *Challenger* had been unable to do was accomplished by Sir Charles Wyville Thomson, chief of the scientific staff: using a microscope aboard the ship, he demonstrated the existence of the Antarctic continent. Although the ship never sighted land, its dredging of the ocean floor yielded rocks of a continental origin which, increasing in number as the ship approached shore to the south, demonstrated the existence of a continental landmass.

As of 1885, meteorologists assumed that the Antarctic greatly influenced the world's weather. They claimed that a constant, large, low-pressure area persisted over the region and that anticyclonic winds blew from the continent. Winters were thought to be less severe than those of the Arctic because of the mitigating effect of the water surrounding the South Polar regions. Scientists understood that knowledge of the earth's magnetic field could not be complete without extensive surveys in the region of the South Magnetic Pole.

Nevertheless, only the vaguest outline of Antarctica had been realized. Merely a fraction of the coastline had been seen and that only at a distance. Despite Maury's theory, scientists were not certain if a continent would be discovered within the Antarctic Circle. Nothing was known of land flora and fauna, for no human had ever set foot on the continent. Scholars assumed either that no life could exist there or that the continent was home to land animals of unknown biological species. As late as the 1890s speculation existed regarding the possibilities for anthropological studies.[28] It remained for the scientific community of Europe to set in motion the exploration of Antarctica.

TWO

From Thought to Action

After James Clark Ross's ships sailed from McMurdo Bay, forty years elapsed before the men of the next expedition viewed Antarctica. In the interim there were some who actively encouraged Antarctic exploration. The plans of Maury and von Neumayer to renew exploration were close to fruition. The stimulation to launch an Antarctic expedition came from three sources: Australian national interests, the international scientific community, and the whaling industry.

In Australia numerous scientific societies joined together to focus on the southernmost continent. The colony was seen as a natural starting point for Antarctic expeditions. Moreover, the depressed Australian economy encouraged adventurous enterprises. In his 1869 address to the Melbourne Geographical Society J. E. Davis (1815–77), second in command of the *Terror* on Ross's expedition, attempted to ignite the interest of the Australian populace and scientific community in Antarctic issues.[1] Although Davis's desire was to open the continent for scientific study, commercial factors were also a consideration, for it was hoped that a new whaling industry would provide a boost to the suffering economy.

In the 1880s E. F. DuFaur spoke at several scientific meetings, noting the influence Antarctica had on Australian weather and suggesting that Australia take the lead in exploration. That theme was continued in an 1884 speech by noted magnetist Ferdinand von Mueller (1825–96), who had been working in Australia and who projected great scientific results from study of the southern regions. He hoped leadership would come from such groups as the Geographical Society of Australasia and predicted commercial gain from fishing, whaling, and extracting mineral wealth.[2]

The Australian Antarctic Committee, eager to promote the commercial aspects of exploration, made an appeal for a whaler from Dundee, Scotland, the leading British whaling port, to take part in Antarctic discovery. The Australians offered a reward for the whaler who brought back a profitable cargo from beyond 60° S or who sighted new lands in unexplored areas. Writing of the work of the Australians, R. A. Swan sees these goals of science and commerce as mutually exclusive. For Swan, Australia's misguided attempt to combine them explained its failure to launch an expedition in the last two decades of the nineteenth century.[3]

The committee sought financial support from the Australian government. Although Duncan Gillies, premier of Victoria, promised help from Melbourne, assistance never materialized. There was no concerted effort to appeal to all the Australasian governments. Even attempts to hold a conference of the various scientific organizations were not successful, and the scientific community could not mount a unified effort to launch an expedition.[4]

A Joint Antarctic Committee of the interested bodies, formed in 1886, worked to attract capital, commerce, and science to such a venture. Cabins for two scientists and their equipment were to be provided on board the whaler. The committee opted for a system of bonuses for any ship owner who achieved certain goals. The captains were to receive extra payment for every hundred tons of fish caught below 60° S. Additional money would be paid for surveys of coastline within the Antarctic Circle, for the establishment of new water routes to the South Pole, and for the discovery of a suitable winter harbor in the Antarctic. Owners could specify a further reward for reaching 70° S, and there were financial incentives for every degree of latitude reached beyond that mark. The funds were to come from the Victorian treasury. The need for such incentives may have stemmed from fear on the part of whalers and sealers to sail in the higher latitudes. Particularly rough seas, which are the norm between 40° and 55°, added to the dangers from ice beyond 55° S.[5]

Several times rumors indicated that an expedition would be launched, but on each occasion the plans fell through when funds were not forthcoming. Beginning in 1887 Baron N.A.E. Nordenskjöld (1832–1901), the

14

noted Arctic explorer, expressed an interest in joining forces with the Australians. Nordenskjöld had completed important Arctic exploration and scientific work in the area of Spitsbergen and was the first to sail the Northeast Passage from Norway to the Pacific across the Asiatic Arctic (1878–80). The association of his name would add credibility to any expedition launched from Australia. Nordenskjöld, who earlier had attempted to gain support for such a venture in St. Petersburg, agreed to come out of retirement to lead the expedition with his son, Erland. The Swedish explorer and the Australians would each contribute a ship and share the costs of the venture.[6]

Baron Oscar Dickson, who had previously underwritten Arctic exploration, offered to donate money toward the costs of the expedition, and a joint Swedish-Australian committee solicited subscriptions. By 1891 Nordenskjöld was expected to leave for the South within eighteen months. The *Spectator* hailed the news of the proposed expedition: "It is but a little garden Man has, and it seems feeble for him not to know it all." The magazine suggested that if other attempts to raise money failed, an interested millionaire should underwrite the scheme. Heads of other colonies such as Queensland and New South Wales committed funds on the condition that the money be matched, but Queensland's parliament refused to approve the appropriation. Although Nordenskjöld continued to correspond with the Australians until 1893, promising and then postponing a launch, nothing materialized. In 1887 the editor of the *Proceedings of the Royal Geographical Society*, doubting that Nordenskjöld would ever sail, suggested that Fridtjof Nansen (1861–1930), the greatest polar explorer in history, might lead the expedition.[7] Although unsuccessful in its goal, the Australian Antarctic Committee undoubtedly influenced developments in Great Britain and Belgium by raising again the possibility of exploration in the South Polar regions.[8]

Meanwhile, on the continent in the late 1870s attention was renewed in polar enterprise, foreshadowing the great surge of Antarctic activity from 1901 to 1904. Karl Weyprecht (1838–81), a German whose interest in naval matters had prompted him to enlist in the Austrian navy, served on two expeditions to the Arctic in the 1870s, the most famous of which was the voyage of the *Tegethoff* (1872–74). With the Austrian explorer Julius von Payer (1842–1915), he discovered Franz Josef Land. Beginning in 1875 Weyprecht called for a coordinated series of scientific polar expeditions. At first concerned mostly with Arctic investigation, the expeditions soon also encompassed Antarctic study. Weyprecht argued that earlier expeditions, although numerous and costly, had produced few empirical results. Previous efforts had been primarily or solely concerned with geographical conquest, and scientific observation had often been undertaken only haphazardly. A series of expeditions was needed that would allow a comparative study of data to give a more complete view of weather, aurora, and geomagnetism. Weyprecht believed that a common plan with coordinated record taking and a joint effort to assemble the data after the expeditions would yield the greatest results.[9]

In 1875 Weyprecht presented his ideas to a meeting of the Association of German Naturalists and Physicians at Graz. There he asserted that geographical discovery was important because it prepared the way for something more meaningful: scientific inquiry. The North Pole, for example, was no more significant than any other point situated in high latitudes. Too much time was devoted to topography, too little to studies that would explain the laws of nature. Observations from different locations which were following the same scientific program, he argued, would yield far more compelling results than those from scattered, isolated stations.[10]

Enlisting Count Hans Wilczek (1837–1922), a veteran of several expeditions in Africa and the Arctic, as a patron in 1876, Weyprecht presented his ideas to the Academy of Sciences in Paris and the Royal Academy of Arts and Sciences in Amsterdam. After Weyprecht gave an address in Rome in 1879, the International Meteorological Congress passed a resolution supporting his ideas. Lacking the authority to implement such a project, this body called for the first International Polar Congress, soon to be termed the International Polar Committee, to meet at Hamburg in October 1879. Eight nations were represented: Austria, Hungary, Denmark, Germany, the Netherlands, Norway and Sweden, France, and Belgium. The congress adopted Weyprecht's plan as its own and elected Professor Georg von Neumayer president.[11]

By the time of the second meeting of the International Polar Committee at Bern (7–9 August 1880), four nations had agreed to establish stations in the Arctic. Because that number was thought insufficient for the intended research, the polar year was postponed for twelve months. Weyprecht died before the Third International Polar Conference met at St. Petersburg in August 1881. There final arrangements were made for scientific observations. The first International Polar Year began on 1 August 1882 and continued through 31 August 1883.[12] During that time fourteen stations—

twelve in the Arctic and two in the Antarctic—gathered information on geomagnetism, meteorology, aurora, and other polar phenomena.[13]

The Germans in South Georgia and the French in Tierra del Fuego established the southern stations. Together they provided valuable intelligence on meteorological and geomagnetic activities. At Tierra del Fuego the mandatory program of observations was supplemented with extensive work in botany, geology, hydrology, and zoology.[14]

The field work of the first International Polar Year was not thoroughly analyzed and published. In 1913 Georges Lecointe, an important figure in cooperative international efforts for Antarctic study, decried the failure to develop the data from the first polar year.[15] Nevertheless, that initial effort drew attention to the need for scientific work in polar regions and presaged the coordinated scientific effort that occurred from 1901 to 1904. Finally, it was an early example of international cooperation for scientific endeavors at the poles.

In 1876 Sir Charles Wyville Thomson (1830–82), chief science officer aboard the *Challenger*, professor of natural history at the University of Edinburgh, and one of the most influential figures in oceanography in the late nineteenth century, spoke in Edinburgh on the comparative conditions of Antarctic and Arctic regions.[16] He argued that the South Pole would probably never be reached because it was hidden behind an icy barrier 230 to 250 feet high and buffeted by high winds and snow. Still, much could be gained for science from a voyage to that region.[17] Among the likely benefits were opportunities to expand scientific understanding of weather and earth magnetism. His efforts had been instrumental in launching the *Challenger*, but now Thomson called for land-based operations far beyond the scope of the ship, addressing issues that would be raised again in the next decade.

Three planned efforts in the early 1880s came to naught. In 1880 a private venture to be led by Sir Allen Young (1827–1915) never materialized.[18] Young, an Arctic veteran who had participated in the search for Sir John Franklin, seemed a likely candidate to lead an Antarctic expedition. He offered to subsidize the expenses of the undertaking, although it was hoped that the Imperial Exchequer would also help with the funding. Sir Graham Berry, the agent general for the colony of Victoria in London, attempted to obtain five thousand pounds from the Victoria government, but because of a lack of enthusiasm in government circles, neither the money nor the expedition was forthcoming.

An Italian Antarctic expedition was proposed by Lieutenant Giacomo Bove (1852–87), who had served on the *Vega* Arctic voyage led by N.A.E. Nordenskjöld. Failing to find financial support, Bove offered his services to the Argentine government and boarded a ship at Buenos Aires en route to Grahamland. The ship was wrecked, but all hands were rescued by a British cutter. At the time, the press mistakenly reported it as a disaster. A second effort by Bove, this time in partnership with Professor Domenico Lovisato, also failed. Meanwhile, the press reported a proposed French adventure headed by M. Mascart of the Bureau Central, but the ship never sailed for lack of funds.[19]

Of the various groups in Great Britain working to sponsor an Antarctic adventure, the British Association for the Advancement of Science (BAAS) took the lead. The association was a quasi-official body devoted to the pursuit and dissemination of scientific knowledge. At its annual meeting in September 1885 Admiral Sir Erasmus Ommanney (1814–1904), a veteran of Ross's Arctic expedition of 1836, urged the renewal of Antarctic exploration. Joining Professor von Neumayer, he stressed the importance of finding a safe winter harbor. His address led to the appointment of a committee to investigate the matter.[20]

The resumption of Antarctic exploration dated from the creation in 1885 of the British Association's Antarctic Committee, which proposed British investigation of the South Polar regions before the end of the century. As in many of the calls for a revival of Antarctic activity, there was a strong appeal to national pride, especially Britain's need to take the lead among "civilized" nations. British cooperation with the colonies in this matter was seen by John Murray (1841–1914) as the "first step in Imperial Federation." Murray, one of the most important figures in nineteenth-century oceanography, helped organize the *Challenger* expedition and, after the death of Sir Wyville Thomson, assumed the herculean task of editing the fifty-volume *Report on the Scientific Results of the Voyage of the H.M.S. Challenger*. When funds for the publication of the report ran out, Murray paid for the printing of the remaining volumes out of his own pocket. Murray was the leading British academic Antarctic expert in the 1890s.[21]

The British Association had played an important role in launching the Ross expedition. Finally, after forty years, the association's Antarctic Committee joined with Sir Erasmus Ommanney in urging new efforts to open the Antarctic to science. Ross's work on geomagnetism required updating to determine how the patterns of terrestrial magnetism had altered in the intervening period because of the movement of the South Pole. Ross's original deep-sea temperature studies had been hampered by instruments that failed under the severe conditions; equipment now existed that could withstand polar extremes. Maury's theory that Antarctic winters were less severe than those in the Arctic needed to be tested, a project that only a wintering station could carry out.[22]

The British Association's Antarctic Committee proposed a naval expedition similar in scope to those sent to the Arctic earlier in the century. It pointed out both the scientific and national advantages of Antarctic exploration and the benefits to be acquired by steam navigation. The BAAS combined its efforts with those of the Australian colonies, principally Victoria, to persuade Her Majesty's government to fund an expedition. The Australian and British Association Antarctic committees worked together to establish the goals of the trip and the means to achieve them.[23]

To persuade the government to join the effort, Ommanney's committee drew up a list of subjects an expedition might investigate and the benefits likely to accrue. Ommanney stressed the need for cooperation among the scientific communities, and the committee, understanding the importance of gaining the support of these groups, sought to include representatives from other agencies: the Royal Geographical Society, the Royal Colonial Institute, the Royal Scottish Geographical Society, and the Royal Society. The council of the Royal Scottish Geographical Society unanimously passed a resolution supporting "the careful exploration of the Antarctic Regions," urging British scientific societies to cooperate with their Australian counterparts. The president of the Royal Geographical Society (RGS) wrote the secretary of state for the colonies to express the RGS Council's support.[24]

In 1886 the Royal Society of Edinburgh created its own Antarctic Committee and invited the colonies of New Zealand and Australia to join it. It also published John Murray's agenda for Antarctic exploration. This document is a remarkable foretelling of the accomplishments of the great international expeditions of 1901 to 1904. In its proposal the committee called for a pioneer ship to scout the ice conditions and determine the best route for the main body. Alternatively, to use more of the summer season the entire group could be dispatched in the spring, in September or October, extending the time for exploring Antarctic waters. Two steam-powered ships would embark, one attempting to winter in Antarctica, the other in Australia, with the latter returning the following spring with relief supplies.[25]

The scientific program Murray planned consisted of extensive dredging to explore the ocean floor. Meteorology was an important consideration; specifically, measurements would be made of wind direction and speed, precipitation, and barometric pressure, to determine if a low-pressure area existed over Antarctica. Barometric pressure would indicate whether there was land all the way to the pole or if a body of water existed between it and the land.[26]

The committee urged that studies of seawater temperature be made, taking advantage of new deep-sea thermometers developed since the time of the *Challenger*. Careful ice measurements would chronicle glaciers and icebergs to help explain the origin of the ice flows, and testing might determine the depth of the ice sheet. More rock specimens were needed to supplement those collected by Ross. Finally, an effort would be made to add to the collection of flora and fauna brought back by the *Challenger*.[27]

The British Association's Antarctic Committee worked throughout 1886 and 1887 to prepare its case. The topic was discussed at the 1886 BAAS meeting in Birmingham, where Ettrick W. Creak read a paper on Gauss's theory of terrestrial magnetism, emphasizing how the lack of data from beyond 60° S hampered study. Murray, rapidly becoming one of the most significant authorities on Antarctic matters, made an important speech at the Royal Scottish Geographical Society in 1886 in which he reviewed the previous British contributions to Antarctic exploration. Urging his countrymen to take up the cause that had been neglected for so long, he implored them to act out of national interest as well as patriotism. The work of the *Challenger* answered many questions but raised dozens more that could be solved only by another expedition, one that would include work on Antarctic land. Ross's collection of animals of the region had never been fully used, and the specimens had deteriorated even before the explorer's return. Geomagnetic observations were needed to complete the magnetic picture of the earth.[28]

Seeking an imperial grant to match the five thousand pounds proposed by the government of Victoria, the British Association Antarctic Committee surveyed various official agencies. The Colonial Office reported favorably, raising hopes that Her Majesty's government would issue the funds.[29] *The Times* endorsed the project, warning that other nations were threatening to steal the lead from Britain: "The home government has scarcely a choice in the matter; a request of cooperation from a powerful colony for the advancement of knowledge can hardly be declined."[30] The Board of Trade saw no benefit in exploration, overlooking the possible gains from whaling and exploitation of Antarctic waters. In early 1888 the Treasury reported unfavorably on the project because it too found no trade advantages. As for scientific inquiry, the Treasury argued that an expedition "on the scale contemplated could do very little in the way of scientific investigation and would have to be regarded simply as the pioneer of future and more complete and costly expeditions."[31] In reaching its decision, the Treasury agreed with the Royal Society, which feared that ten thousand pounds was an inadequate amount. That sum, the society felt, was sufficient only for a small initial venture,

> which, while avowedly not designed to undertake an exhaustive inquiry, would be able, under competent direction, to make a careful survey of the northern boundary of the circumpolar ice region to determine approximately the distribution of open water and the direction of oceanic currents, to take magnetic and meteorological observations, and, by means of the tow-net and the dredge, used at moderate depths, to collect pelagic animals and plants.[32]

Having failed to arouse the interest of the government, the committee was abolished. Nevertheless, together these two committees launched the era of "exploration by committee" which eventually resulted in the *Discovery* expedition (1901–4). Many of the same figures—Clements R. Markham, Ommanney, Murray, and Sir Leopold McClintock—renewed their efforts through the Antarctic Committee of the Royal Geographical Society in the 1890s. The *Discovery* expedition, with Sir Clements Markham as the guiding force, was the epitome of exploration by committee.[33]

In addition to the ongoing Australian enterprise under Nordenskjöld, several others made attempts from 1889 to 1892 to undertake work in the South Polar regions. In Germany, von Neumayer continued his efforts to launch an exploration with the financial support of the government. Henry Villard, a wealthy German-American industrialist, would reportedly either contribute to von Neumayer's efforts or launch his own German-American attempt. Similar accounts of a New Zealand expedition appeared in the press between 1888 and 1892.[34]

The International Geographical Congress of 1891 shed some light on the development of British contributions to Antarctic exploration in the 1890s. The first of a series of congresses that had great influence in promoting Antarctic exploration began in Antwerp with the dedication of a statue of Gerardus Mercator (1512–94) and Abraham Ortelius (1527–98). As part of the celebration a congress convened in Antwerp in August 1871 to discuss geographical matters. From this beginning the International Geographical Congresses developed. Successive congresses met at Paris (1875 and 1889) and Venice (1881).[35]

At the fifth congress, held in Bern (10–14 August 1891), Sir Erasmus Ommanney again raised the issue of Antarctic exploration. The delegates endorsed efforts to launch an Australian enterprise that could do much valuable work. The congresses continued to draw attention to polar matters during the 1890s.[36]

Thus, as the 1890s progressed, there were many calls for an expedition and a demand for scientific data. Numerous scientific bodies in Britain and abroad were involved in the effort to enlist public and private financial support.

In the midst of this whirl of speculation about the Antarctic, Robert Kinnes of Dundee suddenly announced that a commercial venture was being launched. Four Dundee vessels were to spend a season hunting whales. What committees had not been able to accomplish, commerce had.

THREE

Lifting the White Shroud

As has often been the case in Antarctic exploration, commercial gain was the goal of the four whaling adventures of the early 1890s which prepared the way for the scientific expeditions of the second half of the decade. The whaling efforts brought mixed results. Financially, they were modestly successful, although for different reasons than the promoters intended. Their great import was the stimulus they gave to further Antarctic exploration.

The object of their hunt, the whale is one of the most interesting of all creatures. Mammals of the order Cetacea, they are divided into two suborders, those with teeth, Odontoceti, of value only for their oil and meat, and those without teeth, the Mysticeti, valuable for whalebone as well as oil and meat. Of the seventy-five species, sixty-five are toothed and only ten are toothless, or baleen, whales. Although six species of baleen whales are found in the southern ocean, the Dundee whalers sought the southern right whale (*Balaena glacialis australis*). These were literally the "right" whales for whalebone, that rare commodity most often thought of in connection with women's corsets. The substance was also used for buggy whips, umbrella stays, and other commodities requiring a nonrusting flexible material. By the 1890s whalebone fetched an impressive price, £2,500 per ton.[1] The capture of only a few animals could mean financial success for the fleet, as one large whale could yield a ton of baleen.

Southern right whales can weigh up to sixty tons and measure as long as fifty feet. Their habit of breeding in enclosed waters, such as bays, makes them easier to catch than whales that inhabit only open water. Right whales have large stores of blubber that yield a good quantity of oil, which sold in 1892 for approximately £18 per ton.[2]

Baleens range over larger areas than Odontoceti, often covering three thousand miles in their annual migration. Ranging as far north as 30° S, they swim to Antarctic waters in the summer months to feed on the great concentrations of planktonic food, notably krill, the shrimplike creature that forms the base of the Antarctic ecosystem. Krill (*Euphausia superba*) resemble the shrimp consumed by humans, but this appearance is deceiving; the two animals are not related. Krill represent about half the zooplankton found in Antarctic waters, and the survival of all other species in the Antarctic food chain depends on their existence. Krill swarm, becoming extremely concentrated in the water. In the summer months whales are attracted to these concentrations during the feeding cycle. Summer is a critical time, as the whales' winter migration is often undertaken without feeding en route. Right whales survive on stored body fat until they reach food sources in the breeding grounds.

The southern right whale resembles its Arctic counterpart. Its head makes up about twenty-five percent of its body. Whalebone in the southern right whale is shorter than in the Greenland type but serves the same purpose for humans. Unlike the Odontoceti, which use their teeth to capture and kill their prey, the baleens feed by taking in water and using their fibrous plates to strain the food from the water. These baleen plates, approximately 230 pairs of hairlike fibers, are longer than the opening of the mouth and make an effective trap when the mouth is flared slightly to allow water to escape. The whalebone acts like a long, tough, hairy strainer, sufficiently well designed to net even the krill, which average one inch long.[3]

Right whales were relatively easy to hunt because they are slow, seldom making more than five or six knots. By comparison, rorquals—another family of the suborder Mysticeti, including blue whales, fin whales, sei whales, and minke whales—have been recorded at speeds of eighteen knots. Right whales float when dead, but rorquals do not, another factor making baleens somewhat easier to catch, kill, and process than rorquals.[4]

After the first great era of Antarctic exploration (1819–45), whaling declined worldwide because of diminishing whale populations and increased use of alternative lubricants, notably petroleum oil after its discovery in Pennsylvania in 1859. Between 1850 and 1872 the number of whaling ships decreased from more than four hundred to fewer than seventy-five.[5]

Americans, who had dominated the trade in the first half of the nineteenth century, gradually withdrew from Antarctic whaling. The Civil War reduced the number of ships engaged in the activity; ships were confiscated by the Union government to block harbors, and whaling men were assigned to other work.[6]

Before 1850 whalers met with success in sub-Antarctic waters, but their numbers declined as the most easily exploited areas were exhausted. Right whales that had migrated close to Hobart, Tasmania, making it a prominent whaling center, became scarce, then virtually nonexistent.

The Dundee whaling expedition of 1892–93 was not the first to explore Antarctic waters in search of whales. Several American whalers plied these waters during the 1870s; moreover, the *Gronland*, a German steam whaler, ventured south in 1872.[7] In search of right whales it found only rorquals, which were too fast for its crew to capture. Although the men of the *Gronland* secured sufficient seal oil for a modest return on the expedition's investment, the Germans did not repeat the attempt.

Faced with the decline of their business in Arctic waters, whaling men began to consider possibilities in the southern arena, as George Forster, a scientist who had participated in Captain Cook's first circumnavigation, had suggested in the eighteenth century. In the late 1880s whaling had become a less viable proposition with each Arctic season. The practice of sending whalers for two voyages per year ended, and a single voyage became the norm. Fewer cities sent vessels to brave the harsh conditions in the Davis Straits, and the declining whale population meant that captains were forced to sail dangerously close to the ice pack in pursuit of their prey. To some degree seal fishing off Newfoundland was an alternative trade, but only the larger steamers could make that voyage; smaller ships were confined to the Davis Straits run. Dundee whalers continued whaling, with diminishing results, in Greenland and the Davis Straits, supplementing their income by taking seals. Whaling captains agreed that seals and whales were becoming extinct in the Arctic. When attacking a herd of seals, the men slaughtered all, young and old, with no concern for future harvests.[8]

Many believed that right whales could be found if whalers ventured closer to the Antarctic continent where the effects of exploitation had not been felt. However sudden the inception of an Antarctic whaling expedition might appear, it was actually the result of long preparation. What had been lacking, in addition to a willingness to hunt so far from traditional whaling ports, was the motivation to attempt something uncertain. As Arctic alternatives dwindled, it was worth the risk to try southern waters. Earlier reports by explorers of large whale populations in Antarctic seas led to the Scottish expedition.[9]

In Peterhead, Scotland, in 1874 two brothers, David and John Gray, noted whaling captains, published a pamphlet, *Report on New Whaling Ground*. Sent to the Royal Geographical Society of Australasia by the Royal Scottish Geographical Society, it stirred Australian interest in Antarctica during the 1880s. Examining the logs and published accounts of Antarctic explorers, the brothers determined that whaling in the South could be financially viable. The pamphlet reprinted Ross's descriptions of whales in Antarctic waters and concluded: "We think it is established beyond doubt that whales of a species similar to the right or Greenland whale found in northern high latitudes exist in great numbers in the Antarctic seas, and that the establishment of a whale fishery within that area would be attended with successful and profitable results."[10] The *Challenger* had reported sighting whales, but there was no certainty that they remained in those waters or that they were right whales.[11]

In 1892 Robert Kinnes, a Dundee whaling company owner, decided to send four steam whalers to Antarctica to investigate the possibility of reviving the industry by shifting its focus from northern to southern oceans. From the outset it was a purely commercial affair. Underwriting the cost of the venture, Kinnes took a considerable risk. The sailors sensed the risk, and several crew members opted for a larger weekly salary in lieu of a greater share of the profits. The plan was to sail to Antarctica to pursue whales, not to push for a high latitude or to enter the ice pack unless in pursuit of prey.[12] The four ships were steam whalers built to withstand the forces of the ice floes. The vessels were made of oak with sides as much as thirty inches thick, covered with greenheart, an extremely hard wood that had to be worked with special tools and that withstood the scraping blows of pack ice. As the ships lay in port, their sides showed long scars, reminders of the grip of the ice in northern waters. Alexander Fairweather, a veteran of many Arctic voyages, including exploration work, was the captain of the *Balaena*. Captain R. Davidson commanded the *Diana*, while Captain Thomas Robertson, who later led the *Scotia*, the ship of the Scottish National Antarctic Expedition (1902–4) under William S. Bruce, had charge of the *Active*. The smallest ship, the *Polar Star*, sailed under Captain J. Davidson.[13]

From the beginning many applied for positions, particularly scientific places. The owners made no apologies for the commercial nature of the expedition, but the entreaties of British learned societies secured the agreement of the whalers to keep scientific records. Once the trip had been announced, the Royal Geographical Society pushed to include scientific work and offered instruments to enable the four vessels to carry out research with greater accuracy. The ship's medical officers were to be specially trained to make observations and to gather specimens of all types. Through the efforts of Benjamin Leigh Smith, a veteran of several Arctic expeditions, and H. R. Mill (1861–1951), by this time librarian of the Royal Geographical Society and just beginning his long association with Antarctic explorers, the RGS and the government's Meteorological Office provided additional chronometers, compasses, meteorological instruments, and apparatus for measuring deep-sea temperature and gathering sounding data. Mill also prepared instructions for naturalists and for the captains regarding instrument readings and, at the request of Charles Donald, one of the ship's surgeons, suggested an Antarctic reading list. In this way the ships were far better equipped than commercial vessels normally would have been. The captains agreed to record their path and to make meteorological and magnetic observations as frequently as they could.[14]

The ships were refitted for this voyage. The contemporary press made much of a galley that was added on deck to allow the men to sleep in the open during the tropical crossing. A large condenser, capable of distilling five hundred gallons of water per day, was placed on each ship. Unlike later Antarctic vessels, the ships were not reinforced for ice work.[15]

In selecting surgeons for the expedition, Kinnes followed Mill's suggestion and chose for the *Balaena* William S. Bruce (1867–1921). Bruce was greatly influenced by Professor Patrick Geddes at the University of Edinburgh, a leading institution in the area of natural history at the end of the nineteenth century. Bruce had no training and little interest in practical surgery at the outset of the voyage but soon adapted to his role.[16] Through the efforts of Bruce, W. G. Burn Murdoch joined the vessel as assistant surgeon, although his real position was ship's artist. His drawings and sketches combine with the narrative he published to give a good description of the adventure.

The complement of men also included C. W. Donald, who was appointed surgeon for the *Active*, and Mr. Campbell, surgeon for the *Diana*. As interested in science as Bruce, Donald had more opportunity to pursue his avocation during the expedition. Campbell's occasions for scientific endeavors were limited. As was normal in whaling ventures, the men signed on with a fixed pay and the promise of a share of the profits. Salaries were the same as the going rate for northern whaling work. Still, difficulties in finding sufficient experienced Arctic hands delayed departure for two days.[17]

All hands gathered to hear the clerk, who was protected by a solid barrier (useful on paying-off days to prevent overzealous protests on the part of the crew), read at incomprehensible speed the articles that the men had signed. Included were provisions for such varied issues as the food to be served. The men were also very interested in how their pay would be handled in case of shipwreck. In that event the hands wanted to be paid their regular wages until they reached home or at least until they made port. Otherwise, if the ship was lost in Antarctic waters and a month (or as in the cases of Nordenskjöld, 1902, or Shackleton, 1914, several months) was spent reaching a port, the men would be paid only until the ship went down. After that they would be on their own and would be responsible for their passage home. In this instance the men did not win the dispute; their pay would cease with the sinking of the ship.

The scene dockside on East Whale Lane in Dundee in early September 1892 was chaotic. On the streets, which were blackened by the accumulated whale-oil residue from years in the trade, visitors vied for space with barrels of supplies and equipment. As the departure date approached, the ships, recently returned from Arctic waters, were visited by several notables, including Sir George Baden-Powell, M.P., a member of the Bering Straits Fishing Commission, who discussed with Captain Fairweather the future of the fur seal in the Bering Sea and the goals of the *Balaena*'s voyage. The decks were piled with all manner of supplies as the men loaded sea chests and prepared to say farewell to children and wives. Several wives were seen surreptitiously putting coins in the rudder head to bring the ship good fortune.[18]

To the cheers of loved ones on the Tayside, the ships departed separately in early September and made for the Falkland Islands, their first official port of call. Stopping to coal further down the Tay, they had to put off stowaways. More than twenty lads were taken off the *Diana* and the *Polar Star*, and a search of the *Balaena* yielded a dozen more.[19]

The voyage south allowed the men to settle into the pattern of shipboard life. A routine was soon established, varying only with the weather. Strong winds and storms buffeted the ships in the first month (9–29 September 1892), which made for considerable discomfort as the vessels became soggy and dank. Murdoch's account yields glimpses of the lives of sailors in the late nineteenth century, including scenes of them purchasing their work clothes, oilskins, and sea boots from the ship's stores (the cost was deducted from their wages). Bruce and Murdoch had heard enough of the foul conditions and unsavory food of other ships to appreciate that however unpleasant their current surroundings, circumstances were much improved over the recent past.[20]

Sundays were set aside for rest whenever possible, and early in the voyage the sailors felt the ties of the Scottish Sunday strongly enough not to pursue work or sport, but once they had entered whaling waters the toil went ahead without regard to the Sabbath. When seals were plentiful in southern waters, the crew was informed by the captain that killing seals on Sunday was "a wark o' nacesseety." On rest days the crew took care of personal chores, played whist, or read. Among the most popular works were ones that dealt with the Antarctic or with exploration, such as James Clark Ross's account. Bruce developed an interest in Sir Walter Scott, which Burn Murdoch saw as proof "that times were leisurely, not necessarily slow."[21]

On the *Balaena* the first week at sea turned up two more stowaways, William Brannan and Terrence M'Machon, who eventually became regular members of the crew, replacing men who jumped ship in Port Stanley. After that there were few events out of the ordinary. The passing of an occasional ship, which they hailed with the message, "*Balaena* of Dundee, bound for the Antarctic," or the sport of killing itinerant birds broke the monotony. The crew had no hesitation in shooting whatever bird came within range. Not even the albatross was spared; the skin was taken for commercial value, the bones made good pipe stems, and the skin of the feet made a handy tobacco pouch.

Despite difficulties, Bruce conducted scientific work as time permitted. Good weather allowed him to gather in his tow net specimens that he later studied. He persisted in attempts to maintain temperature and barometer readings and to note the flight of passing birds. The captain of the *Balaena* showed no scientific inclination and offered no help, much to Bruce's dismay. While Bruce pursued science, the crew's efforts were more elemental—casting lines or harpooning fish to provide fresh food for Friday dinners.[22]

Days were filled with the hundreds of tasks associated with a ship under sail and preparations for whaling work. The pumps had to be manned half an hour per watch; the work was accompanied by sea chanteys. In addition to his duties, Murdoch painted pictures for the crew or to record the progress of the journey. He also took great delight in listening to the men recall adventures from previous voyages in Arctic waters. Ship folklore led to some time-honored practices, such as celebrating the end of the first month at sea (seen as a month without pay, since the crew had been initially paid on signing), throwing the ship's cat overboard (to end a period of becalmed weather), and tattooing. The weather improved after the cat incident, and in a later period of unfavorable weather the crew wished "for more cats now." Except for Saturdays, every day was much like another. Saturday was named "plum-duff" day by the crew, after the popular pudding that was customarily served.[23]

The tropics brought unbearable heat, conditions the old Arctic sailors particularly bemoaned; the much-touted awning soon became a tattered rag that afforded shade only to those who moved constantly to seek respite from the sun. Crossing the equator (25 October 1892) provided the occasion for the appearance of "Neptune" and his court to shave the heads of all those who had never passed that line before. Neither crew nor scientists were spared this treatment.[24]

For Bruce and Murdoch, days en route to Port Stanley opened with a morning washing in sea water and ended in the evening with a calm pipe. Land was a welcome sight after ninety days at sea, with drinking water becoming scarce. The ship entered the harbor at Port Stanley without a pilot, for none appeared to guide it. Eventually, one arrived to collect the £7 10s. fee.[25]

The stay at Port Stanley was brief, but Bruce used the time to observe the flora and fauna of the island and to gather specimens. During the ship's stay a naturalist who had ventured from England to Port Stanley in search of a position on one of the ships met with the captains but was unable to gain a place. Bruce and Murdoch had a reunion with Dr. C. W.

Donald of the *Active* when it arrived and learned that, except for a brief coaling stop at Madeira, one ship's voyage had been much like the other.[26]

The *Balaena* sailed from Port Stanley on 11 December 1892, and the other ships followed within a few days.[27] Making last-minute preparations occupied the sailors' time as they approached the ice. Within a week they sighted their first iceberg, about half a mile long and "level as a billiard table"; its sides were wave-worn caves "shaped like the arches of a Gothic cathedral."[28]

Murdoch shot the first seal taken during the voyage as it slept on an ice floe. It yielded little blubber. On the 17th a lookout in the crow's nest believed he sighted a bowhead whale, but it proved to be a finner, the sleek rorqual they were incapable of catching. On the 21st the ship's company was divided into three watches of eight hours each, a change from the normal four-hour watches. This schedule would accommodate the possibility of long hours hunting in the whale boats.[29]

By 23 December the two ships were off the Danger Islands, discovered by Ross but not visited since, en route to their rendezvous in the Erebus and Terror Gulf. The *Active* and the *Diana* joined the *Balaena* within four hours of its arrival in the gulf. The *Polar Star* did not reconnoiter at this time and did not meet with the other ships until 9 January 1894. Since it was the smallest and thought to be the least seaworthy ship, in the interim the crews of the other vessels feared that it had foundered. The rest of December and January was spent hunting whales without success. In lieu of whales the captains of the steamers devoted their time to killing seals, the blubber of which they rendered into oil. Dispatching the seals either by rifle or by pickax proved a gruesome affair. The work was constant when seals were present, and scientists and sailors alike participated in the slaughter and preparation of the carcasses. The crew worked enthusiastically, knowing that every seal meant a few extra farthings at voyage's end. Still, it was grueling labor, and all the men suffered cuts on their hands from the work. Sealskins were salted for storage and eventual sale. Despite the difficulties, penguins too were killed and their blubber reduced to oil. Penguins survived blows that would kill virtually any other animal, and a penguin has been known to walk away with an ice ax firmly planted in its skull. Penguins also supplemented the larders of the ships. At one point the ship stopped to replenish food supplies and hunt penguins. Murdoch described the scene:

We dropped a boat with two guns, and shot down the regiment. It was a very sad sight to see the poor beasts shot down; they had not the least idea how to escape this unfamiliar danger. Even when they were wounded and fell down the slippery icebanks into the water, they immediately struggled to get on the ice again to join their companions.[30]

The scientists bemoaned the failure of the captains to pursue scientific work. Bruce used any occasion to gather data, attaching the deep-sea thermometer to the line when the crew took soundings for navigational purposes, but he was continually distressed to be in the midst of such an opportunity for scientific work without being allowed to pursue it. Donald had more chances to gather specimens and was allowed to land on 6 January 1893 in Active Sound at Joinville Island to observe a penguin rookery. Captain Fairweather's interest in animal life did not extend past those creatures with immediate commercial value. Exploring was beyond the scope of the Dundee fleet.[31]

Despite the Scots' efforts, the ships did not encounter any right whales. Carrying orders to stay in the locale where Ross had sighted baleen whales, the fleet crisscrossed the assigned area rather than searching elsewhere. Thus they were limited to an area 60° by 65° S and 51° to 57° W, or a body of water roughly 180 miles by 300 miles. Hundreds of finner whales were seen; their numbers served only as a reminder of the failure of the ships to secure what they had set out to find. Once, in apparent desperation, a man in one of the whaleboats harpooned a finner. As the lines were played out, the rope of another whaleboat was added. The combined lines were made fast to the ship, which the whale then towed, faster than the vessel could move under its own power, for fourteen hours, until the line broke. As the voyage progressed, the Dundee captains believed Ross must have been mistaken, even though that was unlikely, given the obvious physical differences between baleen and fin whales. The commanders did surmise that the right whale might have disappeared from the area in the intervening fifty years.[32]

It is difficult to imagine that experienced hands could have mistaken such obviously different animals, despite the fact that in Ross's day whales were hunted primarily for their blubber; one type of whale was not valued over the others. Still, the rorquals play in the water; baleens do not. Larger rorquals never leap, whereas the right whale does. Various whales feed differently: baleens skim, rorquals gulp. Finally, the blowhole patterns in the two animals are different and their spouts are markedly dissimilar. Possibly, a finner whose dorsal fin was torn away might resemble a right whale, although rights are much broader in the back than finners.[33]

The *Balaena*, the *Active*, and the *Diana* turned northward toward home on 18 February, the *Polar Star* having started back earlier because of the weather and its smaller size. The men of the *Balaena* gave a cheer at the last sight of Antarctic land as they began their three-month return voyage.[34]

During their time in Antarctica, the Dundee whalers had not had the field to themselves. The same pamphlet that motivated their launch had also come into the possession of Christian Christensen, a prominent ship builder of Sandefjord, Norway. Christensen too decided that money could be made in southern waters and dispatched the *Jason* under the command of Carl Anton Larsen (1860–1924), an experienced Arctic whaling captain. Sailing the same month as the Scottish vessels, the *Jason* journeyed from Sandefjord to South Georgia Island en route to the Graham Peninsula.[35]

In Antarctic waters Larsen and his men found no right whales, although they saw abundant blue whales, which they were not equipped to catch. The day after Christmas a chance encounter occurred between the *Jason* and the Dundee whalers. Visits were exchanged, and the captains discussed whaling conditions. Several subsequent meetings took place over the next six weeks. During one, Larsen invited the crew of the *Balaena* to help celebrate their king's birthday. The *Jason* also generously supplied the Dundee men with salt for preserving sealskins, the Scots' stocks being insufficient. Larsen, like the Dundee whalers, turned to sealing to avoid going home empty-handed and was able to fill his ship with seal oil and skins. The *Jason* returned to Norway in June 1893; its first voyage was not a commercial success.[36]

Undaunted by the lack of profit, Christensen sent Larsen and the *Jason* south again, this time with two companion ships, the *Castor* and the *Hertha*. This second trip was intended as a sealing expedition. The large number of rorquals sighted on this venture inspired Larsen, who in 1904 returned to Antarctica to hunt them. In the early twentieth century it became a profitable business, with the use of whale-killing technology not applied in the 1890s. During this second voyage Larsen sailed further south than any previous steamer and made several important geographical discoveries, adding greatly to the knowledge of Antarctic land. Larsen discovered new islands, the Foyn Coast, and Oscar II Land, findings characterized by John Murray as "the most important geographical discoveries in the Antarctic since Ross." He also found fossils, which were the first concrete evidence that Antarctica had once enjoyed a warm climate, and he demonstrated the value of skis in Antarctic terrain, employing them to investigate the lands he visited.[37] On 18 November 1893 Larsen also discovered at Cape Seymour some curious balls of cement and sand that rested on pillars of the same material. He described them as giving "the appearance of having been made by man's hand." [38] Larsen demonstrated how a curious mind could be turned to scientific advantage during a commercial voyage. For his efforts on this expedition, the Royal Geographical Society awarded him the Back Grant. The *Jason* returned to Norway in July 1894.[39]

The last of the whaling efforts of the early 1890s was the brainchild of H. J. Bull (1844–1930), who had emigrated from Norway to Australia. There he became interested in the Antarctic and attempted to form a syndicate of Australian businessmen to explore the potential for whaling in southern waters. Meeting no success in raising money after the Australian financial crash of 1892, he returned to Norway, where he persuaded Svend Foyn, the Arctic whaling pioneer, to fund an Antarctic whaling expedition.[40]

Foyn was born in Tonsberg, Norway, in 1809 and went to sea early in life. After several years in the lumber trade he turned to seal fishing in Arctic waters; his efforts were instrumental in launching that industry in Norway. By 1865 he was wealthy but continued to seek new challenges. Turning his attention to the hunting of blue, or finned, whales, he attempted to overcome the difficulties that had forestalled that business. Finners presented two problems: they were too fast and strong for the small whaleboats used in the capture of right whales, and unlike baleens, finners sank when they were killed. To solve these problems Foyn designed a small, steam-powered whaler that could more closely match the speed of the animal but was large enough to bring in a dead, sinking whale. The wounded animals were still strong enough to drag a fairly large whaler at speeds in excess of eighteen knots for close to a day. To overcome this obstacle Foyn added the exploding harpoon to his arsenal. After the whale was harpooned, an explosive charge went off that killed the animal. The whale was then hauled in on a line that was three inches in diameter. Thus perfected, his invention made him a fortune.[41]

Although Foyn was wealthy, his lifestyle was simple. According to H. J.

Bull, no visitor to Foyn's house ever "had reason to complain of lack of hospitality so long as luxuries were not expected." His known support of ventures brought Bull to ask his help for the proposed Antarctic whaling voyage. The sense of adventure more than profit was Foyn's reason for agreeing to underwrite the project. The elderly man maintained a keen interest in this endeavor.[42]

Foyn purchased the *Cap Nor*, which he overhauled and renamed the *Antarctic*. The barque-rigged whaler had been built in Norway in the early 1870s and registered 226 tons. It had a two-cylinder, forty-five-horsepower engine, making the ship capable of a speed of six knots in calm weather. It was equipped with tanks to store large quantities of oil.

Foyn hired Captain Leonard Kristensen to command the ship. Shared authority, with Bull as agent in charge of the expedition and Kristensen as commander of the vessel, led to friction and divisiveness. Bull considered himself in charge of the journey and complained that his role was not adequately clarified.

> My position towards the Captain was not sufficiently clearly defined for me to feel it within my power to order or command the carrying out of alterations or innovations, however important in my opinion, when they might be considered to strictly belong to the domain of the nautical leader; my suggestions and advice in such cases received very scant attention, to the detriment of our venture.[43]

Similarly, he related that

> as the manager abroad I had great powers, but did not feel that they justified me in interfering in the actual direction of what any capable skipper would justly consider his domain. My scrupulous observance of this self-imposed restriction did not, in my opinion, meet with similar consideration on the part of the Captain.[44]

Painted the colors of all Foyn ships, green with a yellow stripe, the *Antarctic* sailed from Norway in September 1893. Carrying a crew of thirty-one, it was a fully packed ship; for part of the voyage Bull shared his bunk with casks of gunpowder until other arrangements could be made. At the outset the crew was Norwegian, but by the time the ship left Melbourne in September 1894, it carried an international gathering of Danes, Poles, Norwegians, and Englishmen. En route the *Antarctic* stopped at the Iles Kerguelen (19 December 1893 to 3 February 1894), where no right whales were seen but where sealing efforts resulted in a profit of fifteen hundred pounds from oil and skins. The crew killed all the seals in sight, more than sixteen hundred; the slaughter appalled Bull, who had read of but not witnessed sealing operations. He called for international control of the industry, "which must of necessity be intermittent and criminally wasteful in character so long as it is not controlled in a reasonable manner by internationally accepted regulations, as in the Arctic seas, with a view to giving the seals any chance of reproducing their kind." [45] Arriving in Melbourne on 23 February 1894, Bull sold the haul from the Iles Kerguelen and raised additional support for the expedition.

Meanwhile, the *Antarctic* sailed from Melbourne on 12 April 1894 to hunt whales near Campbell Island. During that excursion the ship ran aground on 19 May, necessitating repairs that consumed the profits of the Kerguelen episode; Bull saw this misfortune as "commencing the decline of our lucky star henceforth." Right whales were sighted during this voyage, but the ship was unable to capture them; Bull blamed Kristensen's incompetence. Although there was "no lack of whales around Campbell Island," the crew of the *Antarctic* managed to kill just one. The ship returned to Melbourne on 21 August. [46]

Bull had remained behind at Melbourne during the Campbell Island escapade. Local businessmen indicated some interest in buying out Foyn's share until Foyn cabled his asking price of ten thousand pounds, or roughly double what he had invested in the venture.

Although the *Antarctic* sailed without a scientist, Bull had received some training in meteorology before he left Norway. The RGS had suggested that a scientist be included, and William S. Bruce, formerly of the *Balaena*, was nominated. Unfortunately, he could not reach Melbourne before the departure for the South. Thus the stage was set for the entrance of Carsten E. Borchgrevink (1864–1934) on the Antarctic scene. While the ship was in Melbourne, Borchgrevink applied for a position as a scientist and observer. His family was known to Bull in a general way, which may have aided his application. [47]

The events of Borchgrevink's life to 1894 are somewhat vague. Much of this imprecision stems from his own various accounts. It is reasonably certain that he was born in Oslo of a Norwegian father and an English mother. After a period on the Continent, traveling or studying, he returned to Oslo in 1888 to settle the estate of his father. Subsequently, he emigrated to Australia. He spent four years in the outback at various

Carsten E. Borchgrevink's preferred photograph.
Courtesy of the Royal Geographical Society, London.

jobs, and in 1892 he secured a teaching position at Cooerwull Academy in New South Wales. Learning of Bull's expedition, he applied for a position. After failing in his attempt to secure a place as a scientist, Borchgrevink signed on before the mast.[48]

On 26 September 1894 the *Antarctic* sailed southward from Melbourne. En route the crew attempted to take seals but had arrived too late for the legal season, unaware of the recent New Zealand regulations on the industry. The first berg was sighted on 5 November 1894 at 56° 57' S. The excitement of new territory overcame Kristensen, and he persuaded himself that a new landmass had been discovered, but clearer weather revealed that it was merely a massive iceberg. The 7th of November brought an encounter with an iceberg that damaged the rudder and forced the *Antarctic* to return to Port Chalmers, New Zealand, for repairs. Concerned that word of the incompetent conduct of the expedition would reach Foyn and that the elderly man would order them home, Bull asked the Reuters agent in New Zealand to delay the news of the disaster until the ship had sailed.[49]

Approaching the ice for the second time, Bull's crew reported unconfirmed right-whale sightings. Proceeding south, the men killed seals and spied finners but no baleens. Attempts to catch finners were unsuccessful. Entering the ice pack on 8 December 1894, the ship made slow progress and the crew was demoralized by being imprisoned in the ice. Finally, on 13 January 1895, they cleared the ice and found open sea to the south. A course was laid for Possession Island, in the vicinity of which Ross had reported right whales.[50]

On 19 January a party alighted on the island and observed a large penguin rookery. Borchgrevink made one of the great discoveries of the expedition when he gathered lichen in sheltered areas. Previously, botanists had argued that the Antarctic climate was too severe for plant life. On 23 January the principal accomplishment of the voyage occurred when a landing was made at Cape Adare, the northern tip of Victoria Land.[51]

Although outlying islands had been visited, no debarkation had been made on the mainland in the seventy-five years since the first sighting of the Antarctic continent.[52] As with other aspects of this voyage, controversy surrounds the event. When the boat approached the beach, the captain prepared to step ashore as "the first man." Instead, from the back of the craft Borchgrevink leaped over the side and walked to the shoreline, helping to bring the skiff in but at the same time establishing his own claim to be the first man on the last continent. As a result of this single act, Borchgrevink attempted to build a role for himself in Antarctic affairs in the last decade of the century. His claim was disputed, but the dubious credit appears to be his.[53]

The party walked along the shore, noting that the area appeared to be a good site for a base of operations for a future expedition, as it seemed protected from the elements. Kristensen and the others examined a penguin rookery nearby and gathered stones and penguins. Borchgrevink found more lichen for his collection. Before leaving, the men erected a pole with a box painted in Norwegian colors giving the particulars about the date and the ship. They were on Cape Adare less than ninety minutes.[54]

Their search for whales was unsuccessful. Small Minke whales were captured and finners were seen, but the crew was aware that the hunt for the southern right whale had been a folly. The lateness of the season dictated a turn northward. Bull commented: "The sensation of being the first men who had set foot on the real Antarctic mainland was both strange and pleasurable, although Mr. Foyn would no doubt have preferred to exchange this pleasing sensation on our part for a right whale even of small dimensions."[55] With their backs to the pole, the men of the *Antarctic* moved easily and quickly through the dispersing ice pack. Making a last effort to secure a catch, they considered heading for Royal Company Islands, but as all aboard were eager to return to port, the idea was not pursued. The crew was disenchanted by the failure of the voyage and the friction between Bull and Kristensen. "To the joy and relief of everyone," the coast of Tasmania was sighted on 4 March 1895. Ironically, just before landing at Tasmania, they ran into a school of sperm whales, several of which were taken before a storm interrupted the hunt. After the gale the ship proceeded directly to Melbourne. All were "sick of the expedition and wanted it over"; on 11 March 1895 Melbourne was a welcome sight.[56]

Bad news was exchanged on landing. Bull told those who greeted the ship that the expedition had been a commercial failure and learned that during their absence Svend Foyn had died. The crew returned to Europe by other vessels, and the *Antarctic* arrived in Norway after a five-month voyage.

Bull and Borchgrevink formed a short-lived partnership to launch a second endeavor until a split was caused by Borchgrevink's failure to share credit for the expedition. Bull objected to implications made by Borchgrevink that he was in charge of the *Antarctic* expedition. For example, Borchgrevink related during a speech that on landing at Possession Island, "I addressed my countrymen in a few words, informing them that we were the second party to set foot on the island." The two men parted company. Borchgrevink left for the International Geographical Congress in London.[57]

The middecade whaling expeditions failed in their primary purpose. Any assessment of the research accomplishments of the Dundee whalers must note that science was an afterthought. The scientists were afforded little opportunity for research, although before they left Dundee an ambitious list of achievements had been contemplated. Among the goals was the keeping of full meteorological logs and records of seawater temperature. British scientists had hoped that small surface organisms would be collected and that sea currents would be observed. The expedition had also expected to gather new animal specimens and seawater samples from various depths.[58]

All these projects were attempted by Bruce and Donald, but the results were disappointing. Part of the reason was that the whalers spent less time in Antarctic waters than originally anticipated. Bruce's geological work, for example, was limited to stones found on icebergs and in the stomachs of penguins. The meteorological records that were kept from 28 October 1892 were an important contribution to existing data. The biological specimens were not large in number, but their rarity made them interesting. The erratic scientific efforts led to anxiety that more was not accomplished. Bruce's frustration was evident when he wrote, on sighting what appeared to be the eastern coast of Grahamland, that he was unable "to make further investigation, for our vessel was not yet filled with blubber." Bruce encountered many difficulties, such as the loss of his larger rock specimens, which were thrown overboard by a member of the crew. Simple problems like his inability to replace the bucket used for taking samples of surface water when it was lost on 26 December 1892 hampered his efforts.[59]

The work of Bruce and Donald resulted in greater understanding of Antarctic seals and penguins. Although no new species were discovered, Bruce had an opportunity to observe four types of seals, including the sea leopard, Weddell's false sea leopard, the crab-eating seal, and Ross's large-eyed seal. Bruce observed that the gestation in the region's seals began about December, indicating that most female seals killed were pregnant. He deplored the slaughter and warned that it would quickly lead to extinction of the species. Donald's studies of the penguin contributed to the limited understanding of the species, but the failure to land, except briefly, and the limited area covered at sea severely hampered scientific observations. Donald and Bruce also added greatly to the knowledge about ice conditions and icebergs; the largest one they encountered (on 19 December 1892) was thirty miles long.[60] Bruce described them: "Clothed in mist they raise their mighty snow-clad shoulders to a stately height, or shine forth brilliantly in the sun. Although they are of the purest white, yet they glow with colour. The crevices exhibit rich cobaltic blue, and everywhere are splashes of emerald green."[61]

Clearly, the Scottish whalers failed in their primary purpose. Modern studies show that whale populations do not congregate in the areas where the Dundee whalers were searching. Seals were plentiful and provided income but were no solution to the problem of the dying Arctic whaling trade.[62]

One of the most important results of the adventure was to introduce Bruce to Antarctic work. Bruce was arguably the most competent and best-prepared British polar explorer of the decade. His later expertise truly grew out of this expedition. Burn Murdoch's sketches and drawings provided a more accurate view of the region.

Larsen accomplished more than the Scots, not merely by virtue of a second season of effort but because of his eagerness to explore. Unlike the Dundee captains, he had more freedom in planning his route, and he used that advantage to discover new lands. In Bruce's opinion, Larsen "showed a zeal for extending our knowledge of these regions that would not have been unworthy of the leader of a purely scientific expedition." Still, Larsen regretted that more could not be done: "How interesting it would have been to explore the [King Oscar II] land! but, as we were not sent out for scientific exploration, but for whale and seal hunting, we had to resist the temptation."[63]

Bull's *Antarctic* expedition proved to be more flash than substance. He could point to little in the way of discovery despite the importance of Borchgrevink's finding of the first living organism on the mainland. Although Borchgrevink's efforts at scientific work were handicapped by his lack of training and limited apparatus, analysis by experts of the rocks he collected supported the theory that Antarctica was a continent. Still, the event that stands out is the first landing on the Antarctic mainland. Of relatively little scientific value, it stirred the imagination and launched

Borchgrevink's career as an Antarctic explorer. The *Antarctic* expedition demonstrated two things: that the ice-free water south of the ice pack, reported by Ross, was a normal occurrence and that Cape Adare could be reached during the summer by even a modestly powered steamer.[64]

An evaluation of the work of these three expeditions must note the dangers they faced. The single-ship endeavors were particularly danger-ous, as the sinking of the vessel almost certainly would have meant the loss of all hands. Events of the early twentieth century showed how real the hazard was; a steamer could be crushed in the ice, and seven years later the *Antarctic* actually met this fate. Before these expeditions got under way, rumors spread that the ships might not return and that insurance covered the owners if the ships did not survive. Having four vessels was an advantage only if, at the time of disaster, a second whaler was close enough to react.

These expeditions represented an opportunity to uncover some of the mysteries of the Antarctic. Regrettably, the voyages were largely a lost opportunity. Murdoch reflected:

> And so we returned from the mystery of the Antarctic, with all its white-bound secrets still unread, as if we had stood before ancient volumes that told of the past and the beginning of all things, and had not opened them to read. Now we go home to the world that is worn down with the feet of many people, to gnaw in our discontent the memory of what we could have done, but did not do.[65]

These ventures at least proved that the future of Antarctica would not depend on the right whale. Strangely, Larsen and Bull were among the few to note the opportunities for rorqual whaling. After these three efforts whalers realized that overexploitation of the right whale in tem-perate southern waters between 1841 and 1892 had made this animal virtually extinct in the Antarctic. Even before the first step ashore in 1895 the Antarctic environment had been adversely affected by humans.[66]

Finally, explorers of the 1890s kept interest in the Antarctic alive. Per-haps the great period of Antarctic exploration that erupted at century's end was "set on foot by whaling" and "the newly roused interest in the Antarctic continent at the beginning of the century would have been im-possible without whaling."[67] These expeditions showed that much could be done, but a more concerted effort was needed to launch a scientific endeavor. In England a group of men was conspiring to do just that.

FOUR

No Way South

Even as the three whaling voyages were in southern waters, plans were under way to launch other expeditions. Several ventures ended in failure, but the campaign of the Royal Geographical Society eventually succeeded. In virtually every case there was no further attempt to combine commerce and science: henceforth, science was the sole object.[1] The unsuccessful trials included two by Americans, three by Scandinavians, and one each by a Scot, a Belgian, a German, and an Anglo-Norwegian.

The first American to announce a program was Dr. Frederick A. Cook (1865–1940), whose achievements at both poles have been obscured by the controversy surrounding his disputed conquest of the North Pole (1908–9) and the subsequent legal battles that clouded his later years.[2] Cook, the son of a physician who died when Frederick was five, studied medicine at New York University and established a practice in Brooklyn. A member of Lieutenant Robert Peary's first Arctic expedition (1891–92), on which he distinguished himself for his medical skill and field work, he returned to the United States with a desire for further polar exploits.[3] Proposing an Antarctic expedition, he appealed for support to various groups, including the American Geographical Society, for whom he offered to give a series of lectures to help raise funds for his endeavor.[4] Originally, he planned on embarking from New York on 1 September 1894 to sail to Louis Philippe Land, where he and his staff of twelve, including Peary's Norwegian companion, Eivind Astrup, would winter.[5]

Taking advantage of the reduced price of whaling vessels caused by the decline of the industry, Cook proposed to buy a steamer and sail south equipped for a three-year stay. He planned to adapt Eskimo ways to Antarctic work, employing dogs and Arctic equipment, such as sledges and clothing.[6] He proposed studies in geology, meteorology, botany, and zoology. If conditions permitted, he intended a sledging trek inland while his staff stayed at the coast. His carefully detailed program compares favorably with the work subsequently carried out by the various national expeditions between 1901 and 1904.

The 1894 launch was postponed for a year because of insufficient funding. In the interim Cook toyed with the idea of using a pair of small sailing vessels. A second ship would provide additional security in the event of an accident. When attempts to sail in 1895 and 1896 floundered because of a lack of capital, Cook continued to seek support for the adventure, convinced of commercial gain and the possibilities to advance knowledge in the natural sciences and anthropology. Although he attracted applications for places on the Antarctic expedition, he could not raise the fifty thousand dollars needed to carry out his plans. When Cook finally went south, it was not as the leader of his own voyage but as the medical officer of the *Belgica*.[7]

Few details survive of the aborted attempt by Professor Angelo Heilprin (1853–1903) to reach the South Pole. He was a professor of geology and paleontology in the Philadelphia Academy of Natural Sciences and had been a leader of the 1892 Peary Arctic relief campaign. He hoped to winter in Grahamland, gather meteorological data, and collect specimens of local flora and fauna, but no expedition was launched.[8]

Returning from the Antarctic aboard the *Balaena* in 1893, the Scot, William S. Bruce, lost no time in attempting to secure support for his own polar venture. At the British Association for the Advancement of Science in 1893 he asked for funds for an expedition to South Georgia or some other Antarctic island. To assist him the BAAS appointed a committee with Clements R. Markham, president of the RGS, as chairman and H. R. Mill, librarian of the RGS, as secretary. Toward this goal Bruce acquired promises of financial support from various sources, including a grant from the RGS. Problems developed with Bruce's plan to have a ship land his party and return for the group the following year. Fears that the vessel would be unable to rendezvous with the base camp cooled enthusiasm for the plan, as the scientific community showed less willingness to risk the Scot's life than Bruce himself did. He used the next several years to prepare for later polar forays by participating in Arctic voyages and undergoing further academic training.[9]

H. J. Bull's attempt to launch his second Antarctic campaign was also unsuccessful. He appealed for funds in London as well as Christiania, Norway, but was unable to raise the estimated cost. Failing on his own, he proposed cooperating with others, including Bruce. As late as the onset of the *Scotia* expedition (1902–4) Bull offered Bruce his assistance and tried to secure a place on another southern excursion.[10]

Among Scandinavians who proposed an Antarctic adventure was Fridtjof Nansen, who in 1891 and 1898 considered a voyage south. Each time he was unable to pursue the matter seriously. In 1893 Nansen told John Murray that after his current expedition to the Arctic, he intended to turn his attention to the Antarctic. The dream of reaching the South Pole lingered with Nansen until 1907, when he effectively relinquished his opportunity by loaning his ship, the *Fram*, to Roald Amundsen (1872–1928), Norway's other great explorer of this period. Nansen recalled watching Amundsen sail in 1910 on a voyage that reached the South Pole as "the bitterest hour of my life."[11]

Otto Nordenskjöld (1869–1928) succeeded to the ambitions of his uncle, Baron N.A.E. Nordenskjöld, to mount an effort in southern waters in the mid-1890s but failed to secure the necessary financial support. In the early years of the new century he sailed to Antarctica in command of a Swedish expedition.[12]

Carsten E. Borchgrevink tried for three years to secure funding for an expedition before his plans were at last underwritten by Sir George Newnes, a British publisher. Borchgrevink attempted to capitalize on his experience aboard the *Antarctic* by projecting himself as the man to lead the next expedition south. Within a month of his return to Melbourne, Borchgrevink wrote the Royal Geographical Society asking for money to journey to London and offering to give a lecture before the society, noting, "I have valuable information from those South lands." The RGS was unable to supply funds.[13]

After his talk at the International Geographical Congress in 1895, Borchgrevink proposed to lead an expedition to winter at Cape Adare. Using the cape as his base, he was confident he could march overland to the pole. A subscription list was started, and Borchgrevink announced an extensive program to be undertaken by a party of twelve scientists. In the early stages of his planning he was still trying to combine commerce and science, promising to include whaling and sealing as part of the adventure. Borchgrevink toured the United States for two months in early 1896 to raise interest in his proposal and to acquire funds. During 1895 he announced several times that the money had been secured or promised, but nothing definite materialized until 1896.[14]

As he planned his trip, Borchgrevink expected to sail south in a smaller vessel than the *Antarctic* and to winter at Cape Adare. He emphasized the scientific program, eschewing the drive for the South Geographical Pole. The South Magnetic Pole was another matter. This Borchgrevink did hope to reach, for both science and commerce would profit from learning the exact location of the magnetic pole and from having observations conducted at that site. His ideas regarding equipment were closer to those of Cook than to the views of the later British explorers. Borchgrevink sensibly planned to choose a crew with expertise on Norwegian skis and Canadian snowshoes as well as using Eskimo dogs for transportation. His idea of taking an observation balloon was eventually adopted by the *Discovery* expedition, and he expected to maintain contact with the outside world by means of "letter-carrying balloons."[15]

By 1896, following his lecture tour of the United States, Borchgrevink appeared to have garnered the necessary funding, and in April he informed J. Scott Keltie, secretary of the Royal Geographical Society, that he expected to embark in the fall. Borchgrevink had made an arrangement with J. Gilbert Bowdick of the Commercial Company to have a whaler take the expedition to Cape Adare and pick the members up a year later. In the meantime, the ship could hunt whales and gather guano, for which the Commercial Company had already been licensed. Borchgrevink's group planned a sledging journey to the South Magnetic Pole in addition to work at the coast. Seeking RGS endorsement of his proposed venture, he offered in return to give the society first access to scientific results. He also asked Markham to serve on the honorary council guiding the expedition.[16]

The society's Expeditions Committee recommended approval for Borchgrevink's application. Markham drafted but did not send a letter to Borchgrevink in which he agreed to sit on the council.[17] In late June the project began to unravel as supporters, notably the duke of Westminster, began abandoning the cause. Fearing that the loss of the duke's backing could fatally cripple the enterprise, Borchgrevink appealed to Markham to intervene. By this time, though, Markham had begun to turn against the proposal. At this point Borchgrevink may have missed an opportunity to save the British 1896 Antarctic expedition when he turned down Markham's dinner invitation at Greenwich on the grounds that he was too busy with preparations for the voyage. Learning of this, Keltie immediately urged Borchgrevink to dine with him that night as he was certain Borchgrevink had a satisfactory explanation to give Markham. By refusing, Borchgrevink missed a chance to maintain Markham's support. Writing Markham the next day, Borchgrevink stalled instead of answering his questions about the expedition.[18]

Why this change in fortune? Markham, the duke of Westminster, and others became aware of the details of the arrangements made between Borchgrevink and the Commercial Company. Markham and the others also were distressed by reports that Borchgrevink had dealings with Bowdick before the sailing of the *Antarctic*. In early July 1896 Markham requested that Borchgrevink explain his connection with the Commercial Company and reveal the sources of the expedition's funds. Until satisfactory answers were given, Borchgrevink was not to use the name of the Royal Geographical Society in connection with his venture. Borchgrevink wired back his compliance.[19]

Two days later Borchgrevink provided Markham with details of his dealings with the Commercial Company. He indicated that John Murray had turned against him because Murray feared there was a secret agreement between the company and Borchgrevink, a condition the latter vehemently denied. Borchgrevink assured Markham that if there were anything untoward in his relationship with the Commercial Company he would never have lent his name to the project. Trusting that Markham would continue to believe in him and his enterprise, Borchgrevink implored him to remain a supporter of the British 1896 Antarctic expedition.[20]

Borchgrevink's dealings with the Commercial Company came to an end in July as he unsuccessfully attempted to gain greater control over his portion of the undertaking. He did not immediately abandon the possibility of sailing in the fall of 1896, but lacking underwriting, he faced considerable problems. He urged Keltie not to lose hope that he would embark in the fall.[21]

As the summer progressed, Borchgrevink realized that his chances for an early departure were slim. He began to consider the possibility of joining someone else's expedition, still hoping that the RGS would endorse his plans. He was handicapped, however, by letters Bowdick circulated which indicated the two had had dealings before the *Antarctic* expedition. Bowdick had asked Borchgrevink for notes indicating such a connection, apparently using the correspondence to gain the guano concession. Borchgrevink had indeed written such letters, even though they were not true; he had not met Bowdick until his return from South Victoria Land. Those letters were extracted from Borchgrevink on the grounds that they would be used in "some very innocent and harmless way." Now, however, they were used to discredit Borchgrevink. By the end of August 1896 he had abandoned his idea of sailing that year.[22]

The Council of the RGS finally rejected the idea of supporting Borchgrevink and his expedition, "as certain information respecting Mr. Borchgrevink renders it inadvisable to do so." Relations between Markham and Borchgrevink remained strained from this point, and when Markham wrote his personal narrative relating the history of the *Discovery* expedition, he omitted Borchgrevink's proposed 1896 expedition. At the end of the year Borchgrevink left England for Australia to raise capital for a future venture.[23]

Borchgrevink did not help his cause with the elite in British geographical circles by his involvement in an exchange of letters in *The Times* which aired differences of opinion about his role on the *Antarctic* and his credibility as a reporter. The opening salvo was fired by the captain of the *Antarctic*, Leonard Kristensen, who complained in September 1895 that Borchgrevink had used material available only from the ship's log without giving credit to his source. Kristensen implied that Borchgrevink had overstated both his role on the expedition and his credentials as a scientist. All this was done, the captain pointed out, after Borchgrevink had been given liberty to pursue his personal interests despite having signed on before the mast.[24]

In answering Kristensen's charges, Borchgrevink turned his attention to the president of the Royal Geographical Society, Clements R. Markham. Borchgrevink pointed out several errors in Markham's October 1895 article in *Nineteenth Century* but indicated that William Potter, honorary secretary of the Antarctic Committee of the Australasian Geographical Society, was the real source of the mistakes, particularly the identity of the first person to land on the Antarctic continent. Even though Borchgrevink publicly explained that Markham was innocently mistaken and thanked him for his kindness at recent meetings, the letter prompted retaliation.[25]

Potter responded from Melbourne, charging that Borchgrevink's assertions, although unlikely to be believed, had to be answered because of the publicity given them by *The Times*. Potter was incensed over Borchgrevink's assertion that the former had claimed authorship of an article written by Captain Kristensen. Potter was supported by a resolution from the Australian Antarctic Committee affirming his statements. Publicly, Borchgrevink closed the incident with a second letter in which he claimed to refute Potter's charges, but his defense was ineffective. In the end the exchange of letters did nothing to enhance Borchgrevink's reputation.[26]

Privately, Borchgrevink was fending off other charges. H. J. Bull criticized him and his actions both on board ship and after the return of the *Antarctic* in a damaging letter that reached the RGS. Bull charged that Borchgrevink overstated his qualifications, complained of his treatment during the voyage, and usurped Bull's role as spokesman after the journey. Borchgrevink sensed that Bull's charges distressed Markham and, wanting to protect his reputation, sought Keltie's advice. As secretary of the RGS and a close associate of Markham, Keltie explained that the latter was "an old naval officer and naturally has very decided views on naval discipline." He nonetheless noted that Markham seemed to like Borchgrevink personally.[27]

Borchgrevink refuted each of Bull's charges and countered with several of his own, notably that Bull was a coward and a drunk. Bull's inebriation had been the cause of the split between the two men and was the reason Borchgrevink spoke for the expedition in Melbourne. Cowardice had kept Bull in his cabin during dangerous moments in the ice. Borchgrevink felt that Bull had allowed him to sail on the *Antarctic* to "use me and my work to his ends." Borchgrevink challenged Bull's friends to introduce Bull at the RGS so the Fellows could judge him for themselves. Borchgrevink suggested that Keltie get Captain Larsen of the *Jason* to speak of the character of Bull and Kristensen, as Larsen knew them both. Later Borchgrevink's feelings against Bull eased somewhat, and he asked Keltie not to publicize the letter. Borchgrevink evidently viewed Keltie as a friend and asked him for assistance with RGS matters over the next few years. Keltie apparently retained some regard for Borchgrevink, who translated a book from Swedish to English for him. For the moment

49

Borchgrevink was stymied; he had to wait another year before he could command his own expedition.[28]

Although all these attempts to launch South Polar expeditions failed, in the long run the efforts of the Royal Geographical Society proved successful. Two events began the project that eventually triumphed: the inauguration of Markham as president of the RGS and Murray's address in November 1893.

Markham enjoys an important position in the history of Antarctica. Born in the year of the founding of the Royal Geographical Society, Sir Clements had a career in the navy (1844–52), including a stint of Arctic exploring aboard the HMS *Assistance*, commanded by Erasmus Ommanney and engaged in the search for Sir John Franklin. Leaving the navy, Markham entered the Civil Service in 1853 and served in various posts in the East India Company and the India Office until his retirement in 1877. During this time he introduced the cinchona tree, whose quinine brought relief from malaria, to India. After his retirement Markham devoted himself to writing and traveling. He served the Royal Geographical Society as secretary from 1863 to 1888, editing the *Geographical Magazine* from 1872 until it was merged into the *Proceedings of the Royal Geographical Society* in 1878. He was also secretary to the Hakluyt Society (1858–87) and became its president in 1890. He was elected a Fellow of the Royal Society in 1873 and was created a Companion of the Bath in 1871 and Knight Commander of the Bath in 1896. The fifty volumes he wrote include eighteen biographies and numerous historical works. Occasionally, the quality of his writing suffered, for he "was in all things an enthusiast rather than a scholar." Elected vice-president of the Royal Geographical Society in 1891, he was traveling abroad when, in 1893, he was elected president. His predecessor had resigned as a result of the turmoil that had developed in the society over the admission of women, a measure approved by the council but rejected by the membership as a whole.[29]

Markham's term as president of the RGS was a turning point in British Antarctic developments in the 1890s. From the time of his election to the end of the period under consideration here (1891–1901), the shadow of Sir Clements fell over all British activity regarding the South Polar regions.[30] Markham's perspective in polar matters spanned seventy-five years: he knew many of the veterans of Ross's Antarctic expedition, he was involved personally with Arctic affairs in midcentury, and he knew most of the polar explorers of the first two decades of the twentieth century. An

Sir Clements R. Markham as a young man.
Courtesy of the Royal Geographical Society, London.

inveterate scribbler and a committee man par excellence, Markham was an ideal schemer to launch a great national Antarctic expedition.

With Markham's consistent commitment to Antarctic exploration as a backdrop, the event that initiated British Antarctic efforts in the 1890s was the 27 November 1893 address by John Murray, editor of the *Challenger* reports and the leading British academic authority on Antarctic matters at the time. His speech, demanding a great Antarctic expedition, awakened the British scientific community and helped Markham launch his campaign. In his presidential remarks to the RGS, Markham had touted the upcoming address by Murray as one that would "stir up our enthusiasm as geographers and our patriotism as Britons." [31] In attendance were virtually all the outstanding British figures of Antarctic affairs in the early 1890s, including Sir Joseph Hooker; Sir George Nares; Captain W.J.L. Wharton, hydrographer of the Admiralty; Lord Charles Beresford, political figure and roué; Alexander Buchan; and William S. Bruce.

Murray began by pointing out that nearly all the geographical advances had come from commercially minded maritime peoples. He asked his audience: "Is the last great piece of maritime exploration on the surface of our earth to be undertaken by Britons, or is it to be left to those who may be destined to succeed or supplant us on the ocean? That is a question that this generation must answer." [32] Murray reviewed the history of Antarctic exploration from ancient times, noting that only three explorers—Cook, Weddell, and Ross—had been below 70° S. Beyond that point almost certainly lay a great continent that had barely been explored. The land was not as inaccessible as many reports had indicated. Although covered with ice, which Murray estimated to be as much as 1,600 to 1,800 feet thick, landing and exploring the area now appeared possible. It would be critical to winter there to gather an entire year's meteorological records and to investigate the atmospheric pressure of the area, uncertainty about which was an important weather question of the day. He discussed the importance of the work, saying, "Indeed it is impossible to overestimate the value of Antarctic observations for the right understanding of the general meteorology of the globe." [33]

Much remained to be learned about the ocean surrounding the continent. In Murray's era there was no firm understanding of the Antarctic Convergence, and such questions about the southern ocean were among those an expedition could answer. At the time of Murray's speech no land animal or plant, even lichen, had been found within the Antarctic Circle.

Although Borchgrevink's collections shed some light on life forms in the Antarctic, Murray's point was well taken. While the role of krill and similar animals in the Antarctic ecosystem was understood, much still needed explanation. The *Challenger* had demonstrated the richness of ocean life, but little work had been done in shore areas.[34]

Murray spoke of "the great extent of ignorance concerning all that obtains within the South Polar regions," avowing that all scientific persons admitted that Antarctic exploration would benefit natural science and quoting several scientists to buttress his case. Among the most outspoken was Professor F. E. Schultz, who affirmed that "there is no region on the surface of our globe which is so little known, but so much deserves a thorough investigation as precisely this of the Antarctic."[35]

Having established need, Murray then explained what the program of a proposed expedition should be:

> To determine the nature and extent of the Antarctic continent; to penetrate into the interior; to ascertain the depth and nature of the ice-cap; to observe the character of the underlying rocks and their fossils; to take magnetical and meteorological observations both at sea and on land; to observe the temperature of the ocean at all depths and seasons of the year; to take pendulum observations on land, and possibly also to make gravity observations at great depths in the ocean; to bore through the deposits on the floor of the ocean at certain points to ascertain the condition of the deeper layers; to sound, trawl, and dredge, and study the character and distribution of marine organisms.[36]

How was this program to be accomplished? Polar science would be served not by a dash to the pole but by careful and systematic examination of the area. Murray argued that the exploration should be conducted by the Royal Navy. He called for two ships to be fitted out and two parties landed on the Antarctic continent, one in Grahamland, the other in McMurdo Bay. He conceded that the wintering parties could be composed of civilians, an issue that would have great importance in the 1899–1901 period. Murray did not hold out the promise of financial gain for the backers of a scientific endeavor. He saw no reason to hope to profit from right whales or piles of guano.

In the discussion after the address several interesting points were raised. Sir Joseph Hooker, one of the last survivors of the Ross expedition, pointed out that a great deal had been accomplished by Ross and Weddell, though both explorations had been the result of fortuitous circumstances, not careful planning. Weddell had found himself in open seas quite by the accident of unusually favorable summer weather. Ross had been primarily involved in magnetic observations and, while seeking the South Magnetic Pole, had passed through the ice pack and discovered Victoria Land, which forestalled his efforts to reach his goal. A well-prepared expedition would certainly accomplish much more. Hooker stressed that before a great assault was launched on land, additional time, perhaps the whole first season, should be spent surveying coasts and seeking new water routes to the pole.[37]

The duke of Argyll, president of the Royal Scottish Geographical Society, voiced his enthusiasm for the project, noting that the Antarctic was far more likely to yield new insights than the Arctic. Emphasizing the importance of glaciological issues in geology, he stressed the wonderful opportunity Antarctica represented for studying the movement of ice. Urging his countrymen to take up the challenge, he stated:

> I always feel a little shame that civilised man, living on his little planet—a very small globe—should, in this nineteenth century of the Christian era, not yet have explored the whole of this little area; it seems a reproach upon the enterprise, civilisation, and condition of knowledge of the human race.[38]

Argyll was joined by Sir George Nares, commander of the *Challenger*, in disagreeing with Murray regarding the potential commercial value of Antarctica. Citing Murray's allusion to the wealth of fish in southern oceans, he argued that angling alone could be of great commercial importance. Nares commented on the cost to the government and the benefits to the navy of such a voyage and insisted that the navy could spare the men.[39]

Sir R. Vesey Hamilton, who had the honor of being the only other person in the previous forty years to address the society on the Antarctic, enlarged on the theme he had taken up earlier—namely, that a steam-powered ship could accomplish in one season what had taken Ross three years. Freed of the danger inherent in depending on the wind in ice-filled seas, the party would find it easier to navigate and work. Hamilton, a navy man, urged that the work be taken up by the navy but hoped that a scientific staff, as on the *Challenger*, would be employed in the proposed venture.[40]

British glory was cited by several speakers as another reason to launch a national expedition. Captain W.J.L. Wharton averred that the *Challenger* effort was envied by other nations and that Britain, which "has ever led the way in exploration in all climates and all seas," should pursue further Antarctic work "for sure science [and the] redounding credit of England through the whole civilised world."[41]

After Murray's address the Council of the RGS appointed an Antarctic Committee to report on the best means to achieve Murray's objectives. Named to the committee were Hooker, Nares, Wharton, Hamilton, Admiral Sir Erasmus Ommanney, Arctic explorer Benjamin Leigh Smith, Murray, and Markham. From the outset the strong naval influence in the committee was evident, and in the long run that led to problems. For now it was trouble enough that they underestimated the difficulties they faced, believing as Markham did that "if men of science are unanimous, both as to the importance of the work and the best method of executing it, and if they are backed by enlightened public opinion, the Admiralty will be only too glad to take the subject into favorable consideration."[42]

When the committee reported its findings on 7 December 1893, it listed magnetic work as the most pressing need, citing von Neumayer's comment that "the next important step in the study of terrestrial magnetism cannot be taken until further observations have been obtained from the Antarctic regions." Beyond that, marine biology, deep-sea dredging, and studies in sea temperature were paramount. Naturally, the committee pointed out the geographical opportunities in a vast, unexplored land. The committee wanted the venture "to determine the extent and nature of the Antarctic continent" and remarked that little was understood about the ice pack girding the land, a barrier that at the time had been penetrated only once. The report called for the dispatch of two ships and estimated that three years would be required in the South Polar regions. Finally, the committee reminded the council of the benefits to the navy and to national pride which would accrue from this effort.[43]

Markham's attempt to launch a national Antarctic expedition was made in the context of earlier trials. Three times previously in the nineteenth century, scientific agencies had successfully lobbied the government to back an expedition. In the first case, the efforts of the British Association for the Advancement of Science to promote the Ross expedition, a guiding spirit, Sir Edward Sabine, had pressed the organization to act. The BAAS was the promoter of the scheme, and the timely intervention of Northampton, president of the Royal Society, clinched the matter. Interestingly, a previous attempt by the society to achieve the same goal had failed because "it lacked relentless manipulation and authoritative leadership."[44]

The second case began in 1868, when Sherard Osborn (1822–75), a veteran of several Arctic searches for Sir John Franklin, read a paper at the Royal Geographical Society calling for an expedition to the North Pole. The society supported this cause, at first unsuccessfully. Then the RGS joined the Royal Society to persuade the government to fund the venture. The effort was guided by a committee composed of Osborn, F. L. McClintock, and G. H. Richards, with Markham, a member of the Council of the RGS since 1862, having a hand in the project. Two ships, HMS *Alert* and HMS *Discovery*, under the command of Captain Nares, sailed in May 1875. The voyage achieved moderate results but failed to reach the North Pole. The reason for the limited achievements are important.

> In retrospect, its lack of greater success is hardly surprising. The restraining hand of the Arctic veterans on the organizing committees, Markham among them, ensured that the expedition was almost a carbon copy of those fine old expeditions of the 1850s, with little advance in either equipment or technique.[45]

This experience presaged many of the problems of the *Discovery* expedition of 1901–4.

In the third case Wyville Thomson, professor of natural history at Edinburgh, persuaded the Royal Society to petition the government to support an endeavor to study marine biology. William Gladstone's cabinet responded enthusiastically, and the result was the voyage of the *Challenger*.[46] The *Challenger* expedition opened an entire branch of scientific discovery—the physical geography of the ocean—establishing Britain's lead in this field and demonstrating the value of government involvement in research.[47]

Aware of these previous experiences, Markham attempted to enlist the support of the Royal Society for his new Antarctic effort. On behalf of the RGS, he wrote the Royal Society on 20 February 1894, asking the group to assist in taking "the lead in approaching the Government in this subject."[48] The Council of the Royal Society appointed a committee made up of Sir Joseph Hooker, Sir J. Kirk, Sir John Lubbock, and Captain W.J.L.

Wharton to look into the matter. Nearly a year passed before Michael Foster, secretary of the Royal Society, responded to Markham on behalf of the council.

During that time the Royal Society's Antarctic Committee reported that "the investigator continually finds his progress barred by want of knowledge of the conditions existing in the large area in the Southern regions." Even though work in the Arctic had answered many questions about that part of the world, the difficulties encountered in southern oceans were so great that they hampered individual effort. Magnetic studies had been particularly stymied. One of the most pressing questions was whether the magnetic poles were stationary or revolved around a given point. Although it was not critical to reach the South Magnetic Pole, several years of work in the vicinity was needed to solve the remaining mysteries of global magnetism, information discoverable only in Antarctica. Similarly, the oceanographic investigations begun by the *Challenger* required further studies, and gaps in meteorological knowledge could be filled only by additional Antarctic data. Moreover, much would be added to science's understanding of geology and geography: "The celebrated voyage of the *Challenger* added a far greater store of knowledge to all sciences than was contemplated by the most sanguine of its promoters, and it cannot be doubted that an Antarctic Expedition would similarly open up fresh avenues to science." The committee estimated the cost of building and equipping two suitable ships and supporting them for three years at £180,000. It left to the council the question of when to petition the government.[49]

In November 1894 Foster informed Markham that although the council felt there were "forcible reasons for the immediate undertaking of such an expedition," this was not the time to approach the government. During that year the Royal Society questioned officials about support and found little. In July 1894 Foster asked the Lords of the Admiralty to receive a deputation from the Royal Society on this matter, but the meeting failed to elicit government support for Antarctic research. Markham bemoaned the lost year and complained that the Fellows of the Royal Society had approached Treasury officials on their own. Although this first attempt to enlist the Royal Society in the cause failed, Markham resolved to appeal to other learned societies to build a case for a national Antarctic expedition. When the plans were developed, Markham argued, money would be forthcoming. Throughout the remainder of the decade he spoke whenever possible to organizations throughout Britain to promote Antarctic exploration.[50]

As president of the RGS, Markham launched his correspondence campaign to various scientific and geographical societies in December 1894. In his letters he reviewed events of recent months, starting with Murray's November 1893 address. He related that the Royal Society's Antarctic Committee, after looking into the matter, had reported the need for further research, but that the initial inquiries of the society had foundered on the question of the government's ability to underwrite such an effort. Markham argued that money was irrelevant at this early juncture; besides, the initial projections may have been unduly high. It would be better for estimates to come later, after the united scientific bodies could present more accurate figures. First, agreement was needed among the scientific organizations that the renewal of Antarctic research was of vital importance. Markham called on all agencies to turn their attention to the issue of exploring the South Polar regions and to unite to form such an expedition.[51]

Markham began receiving replies in early January 1895. Most were favorable, agreeing with his ideas and often enclosing a supporting resolution. The one from the Zoological Society of London is typical: "That a renewal of Antarctic research is of great importance to science, and that such an expedition as is proposed should be undertaken at an early date."[52]

Many organizations not only expressed their support but offered to assist in designing a scientific program for their area of interest. Occasionally, a reply was unfavorable, not so much to the idea of further Antarctic research but to Markham's proposed method of achieving the scientific goals of the project. Most important, several societies subscribed funds.[53]

Letters and speeches were not the only means by which Markham promoted South Polar activities. He hoped to use the Sixth International Geographical Congress to further his cause. The RGS hosted the event, which met in London from 26 July through 3 August 1895 and brought together geographers from around the world. The gathering meant a great deal of work for the society, with most of the responsibilities falling on J. Scott Keltie, the secretary, and H. R. Mill, the librarian.

Two incidents at the congress dealt with the Antarctic. On 1 August it turned its attention to exploration, with special consideration of the

Antarctic. Borchgrevink spoke on the results of his recent journey on the *Antarctic*. Although his brusque manner offended some, the immediacy of his information and his enthusiasm electrified the audience. Here stood a man who had just returned from the South and was eager to go again. He proposed to lead an expedition to winter at Cape Adare, a site approved by Murray.[54]

The congress then took the oft-mentioned step of resolving on the motion of H. R. Mill

> that the Congress record its opinion that the exploration of the Ant-
> arctic Regions is the greatest piece of geographical exploration still
> to be undertaken. That, in view of the additions to knowledge in
> almost every branch of science which would result from such a
> scientific exploration, the Congress recommends that the scientific
> societies throughout the world should urge, in whatever way seems
> to them most effective, that this work should be undertaken before
> the close of the century.[55]

Thus the most important international geographical organization had called for the renewal of Antarctic research.

Soon after the International Geographical Congress, Borchgrevink had another opportunity to promote his plans for a return to Cape Adare. At the annual meeting of the BAAS at Ipswich on 13 September 1895 he reminded his audience of his intention to take advantage of the commercial assets of the area, such as whales, seals, minerals, and guano. The response was mixed. Although his lantern slides reminded Sir Joseph Hooker of what he had seen with Ross, Sir William Flower deprecated Borchgrevink's attempt to combine science and commercial gain.[56]

Having prepared the way with endorsements from scientific agencies throughout Britain and with the approval of the International Geographical Congress, Markham thought it a suitable time to approach the government. He wrote G. J. Goschen, first lord of the Admiralty, requesting that a deputation be allowed to meet with government officials to present arguments for a Treasury-supported Antarctic expedition. Goschen refused to meet with the group because official support for such a venture was out of the question.[57]

Thus far no one had succeeded in arranging the assistance necessary to launch a new Antarctic venture. Markham's cause appeared finished in

November 1895, in view of the government's refusal to provide support. With the decision of the Expeditions Committee of the RGS in January 1896 that the time was not right to attempt an Antarctic campaign, Markham's fortunes were at a low ebb. Yet within three years two separate expeditions were sailing south and Markham's efforts were renewed.

FIVE

Toward the National Expedition, 1896–1899

During 1896, when it appeared that Carsten E. Borchgrevink might successfully launch an expedition, Sir Clements R. Markham and the Royal Geographical Society declined to pursue their own project. After Borchgrevink's plans fell through, Markham encouraged the society to promote an Antarctic enterprise.

In November 1896 Markham met with G. J. Goschen, first lord of the Admiralty, the same office he had held twenty years earlier when he had assisted in the launch of the *Challenger*. Sir Clements followed that conference with a letter appealing for Treasury support. Reviewing the need for such an undertaking, he cited the benefits of government monies, reiterating his conviction that the effort should be led by naval officers. Though he recognized that state sponsorship was unlikely, he argued that precedents existed for a government grant to support an expedition sponsored by the society. The cabinet's refusal in 1888 to fund South Polar research had been based on the lack of commercial possibilities, but now Markham proposed a purely scientific campaign, subsidized by the Treasury. The president of the RGS anticipated that an imperial grant would encourage colonial governments to contribute. Markham also asked for the loan of naval officers for his campaign, noting that previous requests had always been granted. He stressed the benefits that polar experience gave naval personnel and noted: "Alike in the days of Cook, as it was in the days of Ross, Antarctic work has always been undertaken by the Government, and is strictly naval work."[1]

Like the first appeal, in the late 1880s, this one was rebuffed. In early 1897 H. Vansittart Neale, assistant secretary of the Admiralty, explained to Markham that while the Lords Commissioners of the Admiralty recognized the scientific importance of the enterprise, they could not take any direct part in its support. Not only did they deny funds, but they also turned down Markham's request for the loan of naval officers. Faced with a second refusal from the government, the Expedition Committee of the RGS called for the society to take the lead in Antarctic exploration. Any expedition without Treasury backing would be "deprived of numerous advantages," but an independent undertaking was the best alternative. In April 1897 the Council of the RGS resolved to begin such an effort and, to show its determination and good faith, subscribed five thousand pounds to the Antarctic Fund.[2]

The society then wrote to institutions and individuals explaining the purpose of the project and asking for financial support. Markham pointed out that the Queen's Jubilee year, 1897, was a fitting time for this effort: "As the geographical history of the Queen's reign commenced with an Antarctic exploration, so the sixtieth year from Her Majesty's accession should be worthily commemorated by preparations for continuing the exploration of that southern continent which bears the name of Victoria."[3]

In his addresses and writings Markham repeated the themes he had been stressing since becoming president of the society. In addition to national pride, which remained a basic tenet in his advocacy of this endeavor, Sir Clements focused on three principal benefits of an Antarctic expedition: exploration would yield important results in all branches of science, the benefits from the study of terrestrial magnetism were particularly important, and no better training ground existed for British naval personnel than the polar regions. The old navy man believed strongly that his former service would be a prime beneficiary of exploration in South Polar waters.[4]

Markham used the Jubilee to promote his cause by inviting colonial premiers to a meeting at the Royal Geographical Society on 5 July 1897. Several accepted, but unfortunately none attended, because of other engagements.[5] Undaunted, Markham went ahead with the presentation. The gathering reflected his hope of colonial, especially Australian, support for the cause. The society had assisted in the exploration of Australia, and now the time had come for colonials to help with the conquest of the Antarctic. The Australians, he argued, stood to gain the most financially from such endeavors, and both countries would benefit from work toward a common goal; such an effort would show the two to be "one people with the same interests and aspirations." Markham hoped that half the cost of the expedition could be raised from colonial legislatures.[6]

At the meeting various authorities presented the case for further exploration. The need for magnetism studies and geographical discoveries was prominently cited. John Murray, who was unable to attend, wrote as a fellow colonial, reminding the group that "the acquisition of new knowledge is of great interest to all progressive peoples."[7]

Representatives of the Australian colonies were asked to speak. Sir Saul Samuel, agent-general for New South Wales, mentioned the revival of whaling as a positive result of further exploration, and Sir Andrew Clarke, agent-general for Victoria, reminded the audience that he had long been an advocate of Antarctic activity. The meeting was closed by the marquis of Lothian, who sounded a patriotic note:

> I should, too, like to say one word, which I think would appeal to many people, and that is, that the work of Antarctic research should be done by Englishmen. Looking at the map which hangs before me, it strikes me that almost every name in the south has been given by this country. I know that foreign countries are at this moment striving to inaugurate expeditions in order to discover what we ought to try and do ourselves. I should not like to see foreign names upon that hemisphere where all civilized points are inhabited by our countrymen and belong to this country. Therefore, though I am not urging the work upon you from so high a level as that of science, still I think that our historical record in all parts of the world, which has been begun by Great Britain, should not [be allowed] to fall into the hands of others. We cannot expect to do all, but we should be first in the field.[8]

Despite the optimistic tone of the meeting, the results were disappointing. Queensland's legislature—the only one that responded to the call—contributed one thousand pounds. Throughout 1897 little progress was made in raising money. In spite of Markham's appeals, he had small success in arousing support. While requests to the public continued, Markham renewed his attempts to gain a government grant, writing in October 1897 to the prime minister, Robert Cecil, Lord Salisbury, to argue his case. Markham listed several examples of previous grants-in-aid and expressed hope for similar backing. He reminded Salisbury that the prime minister had been president of the British Association for the Advancement of Science in December 1894 when that body recommended the dispatch of an expedition to the South Pole. Now other nations were stealing Britain's lead. Germany was gathering funds for an expedition, and Belgium already had a ship fitted out and ready to sail. Markham argued that it was not the time for "our country, so long the mother of discovery and of maritime enterprise, to abdicate her leading position." If the government would supply the money, the effort could be guided by a special committee and staffed with capable individuals who were ready to depart.[9]

Once again Markham's appeal was refused. Salisbury regretted his inability to grant the request, adding that he was "unable to hold out any hope of Her Majesty's Government embarking upon an undertaking of such magnitude."[10]

Late in 1897, with progress agonizingly slow, Markham again turned to the Royal Society for assistance. The Fellows thrust themselves into the fray by holding a special meeting on 24 February 1898 devoted to describing the scientific advantages of Antarctic exploration. In the audience, in addition to leading London scientists, were two of the continent's doyens: Fridtjof Nansen and Dr. Georg von Neumayer. The meeting was opened by John Murray, who resumed the themes of his November 1893 address.

Murray argued again for the benefits that would accrue from meteorological and magnetic studies and called for two years of systematic research in southern waters. The expeditions of the past five years had shown that the continent was not unassailable, as once had been thought. He asserted that a party stationed at Cape Adare could answer many scientific questions, for at that time the amount of information on all Antarctic matters was so limited as to make all generalizations hypothetical.[11]

The meeting was an exceptionally long one, as the luminaries of British science and exploration followed Murray to the podium. Each focused on an area of particular interest: the duke of Argyll commented on the possibilities for the study of glaciology; Sir Joseph Hooker spoke of the lands open for geographical discovery; and Dr. Alexander Buchan, secretary of the Scottish Meteorological Society, asserted the necessity of further meteorological research. Several speakers, including W.J.L. Wharton and Murray, expressed their hope that this would be a naval expedition. P. L. Sclater, secretary of the Zoological Society, addressed the need for further work in identifying Antarctic fauna. Reminding his audience that most of the extant zoological specimens had been gathered by James Clark Ross half a century earlier, he stressed that more knowledge of animal life was needed. Knowing which now-extinct animals had once lived in the Antarctic would shed light on the history of its climate.[12]

Nansen asserted that Britain was the most likely nation to undertake Antarctic exploration. Although inland penetration would be difficult, he assumed that the land's surface would be smoother than Greenland's and thus easier to traverse. Contending that Antarctic weather had an enormous impact on global climate, he added that if Britain dispatched a vessle, Norway would send a group to cooperate with the British.[13]

Von Neumayer praised previous British exploring activities and urged international cooperation to establish stations to gather data. He pressed his audience to pursue research in terrestrial magnetism. Studies in this field, he asserted, were "positively at a standstill" for the lack of Antarctic data.[14]

Supported by the Royal Society, Markham continued to speak and write on behalf of his project. Throughout 1897 few offers of assistance were received, and at year's end only twelve thousand pounds had been raised. Most of that amount came from the RGS and from a gift of five thousand pounds from Alfred C. Harmsworth, a publisher who had previously underwritten the cost of the Jackson-Harmsworth Arctic expedition.[15]

While Markham struggled to raise the hundred thousand pounds he estimated was needed for a British assault on the continent, a small expedition was launched for roughly one-tenth that amount. Adrien de Gerlache (1866–1934), a Belgian naval lieutenant, began in the 1890s to contemplate an Antarctic undertaking. He offered his services to N.A.E. Nordenskjöld, but when the latter's plans did not materialize, Gerlache began making his own arrangements. While Markham was having difficulty attracting money, Gerlache raised the more limited funds he sought. The Belgian Geographical Society became a patron of the project in November 1894 and organized a national subscription in Gerlache's behalf. It was a true grassroots campaign, with donations from collections at county fairs as well as from the wealthy. At a critical moment just before sailing, when a lack of funds threatened to halt the effort, the Belgian government supplied sixty thousand francs. In the end Gerlache raised roughly three hundred thousand francs (approximately twelve thousand pounds), a fraction of what Markham sought but sufficient to fund a smaller expedition.[16]

Gerlache intended to sail in the late summer of 1897 to South America and from there to the ice. His plans called for exploring as far south as possible during the first summer, with the vessel returning to winter at Melbourne. The second season would involve an attempt to reach the South Magnetic Pole. At no time before the launch was there a public statement about wintering in the Antarctic.[17]

Gerlache's intentions have been the subject of much speculation—namely, that although it was never stated so publicly, the Belgian intended all along to winter in Antarctic waters. Aboard ship some surmised that this was his plan. During the time that the expedition was overdue at Melbourne, the *Geographical Journal* reported that Colonel de Gerlache, Adrien's father, suggested that a change of plans may have occurred and that provisions were carried aboard for three years. Crew member Henryk Arctowski complained that the entire expedition lacked an overall plan.[18]

In Norway in February 1896 Gerlache purchased a steam whaler, the *Patria*, which he refitted and rechristened the *Belgica*, a three-masted barque of 25 tons, 30 meters long and 6.5 meters abeam, powered by a 150-horsepower engine. A weakened market depressed prices, and Gerlache was able to acquire the ship for only fifty thousand kroner. Built in Drammen in 1884, the *Belgica*, typical of the whalers of the time, was constructed of oak with an outer covering of greenheart. Using sails supplemented by a small engine, the *Belgica* could make six to seven knots.[19]

Gerlache spent the winter of 1896–97 in Norway preparing for the expedition, learning to ski, and gathering information about materials and equipment. The ship was being refitted in Sandefjord, and Norway was the natural locale for Gerlache's training because of the climate and the Norwegians' superior knowledge of skiing. As the preparations continued, Gerlache received visits and suggestions from Markham, Nansen, and others interested in polar affairs.[20]

The *Belgica* expedition was a fugue in seven voices. Although most of the communication was in French, other languages spoken included Flemish, Norwegian, Polish, Romanian, Russian, and English. Gerlache's polyglot crew included the Belgian Georges Lecointe, who served as executive officer and hydrographer; the Norwegian Roald Amundsen, later conqueror of the South Pole, as first mate; the Belgian Emile Danco (1869–99), magnetician; the Romanian Emile Racovitza, naturalist; the Pole Henryk Arctowski, geologist, oceanographer, and meteorologist; and the Russian Antoine Dobrowolski, assistant meteorologist. Just before sailing, the medical officer resigned. Four thousand miles away in Brooklyn, Frederick A. Cook, who had unsuccessfully attempted to launch his own project, read of this problem in the newspaper and cabled his application for the position. He was accepted, sight unseen, and instructed to meet the *Belgica* in Rio de Janeiro. Cook was the surgeon, anthropologist, and photographer. The crew served without pay.[21]

Sailing from Antwerp in August 1897, the ship arrived in Rio de Janeiro on 22 October. Cook joined the crew, and the *Belgica* then sailed down the remainder of the South American coast surveying the shoreline. The vessel departed from Punta Arenas on 14 December for further charting. It was not until mid-January—late in the season for exploring—that the expedition left South America for Antarctic waters. Time was invested in surveying the Hughes Bay area, and the *Belgica* did not enter the Pacific en route to Antarctica until 12 February 1898.[22]

The men charted several islands off the coast of Grahamland—Brabant, Anvers, and Liege islands—and continued south, crossing the Antarctic Circle on 15 February. Even at this late date Gerlache was determined to establish a new furthest south and pushed the tiny whaler into the ice pack. The scientists questioned the wisdom of this decision, preferring to use their time to explore nearby islands; nevertheless, the *Belgica* continued until 3 March, when its path was blocked by ice. For one week the explorers attempted to extricate the ship, but by the 10th they were trapped in the ice.[23]

Realizing that they would have to winter aboard, they prepared the vessel for the ordeal. All scientific observations were continued, and studies were begun of the ice and the remaining leads of open water. The ship was made as habitable as possible, and all drafts were sealed to conserve heat.[24]

After the sun set on 17 May, it was not seen again until 23 July. As the Antarctic night set in, the crew members became melancholy and despondent. During those dark weeks lethargy and illness caused by poor diet threatened their lives. Their tinned food lacked vitamins, and the men grew tired of the soft, mushy meals. In July the *Belgica* lost a second member of its crew when Lieutenant Danco succumbed to heart failure. In January a sailor, Carl Wiencke, had been washed overboard and drowned. Several men showed signs of insanity, and most were incapacitated in one way or another.[25]

It was Cook who saved the men's lives. Because his Arctic experience had taught him the benefits of fresh meat, as medical officer he ordered a change in diet. Early on, seal and penguin had been tried but rejected as inedible. Cook's description of penguin reflects the crew's feelings: "If it is possible to imagine a piece of beef, an odoriferous codfish, and a canvas-back duck, roasted in a pot, with blood and cod-liver oil for sauce, the illustration would be complete." Cook persuaded Gerlache and the others to eat both seal and penguin and thus ingest needed vitamins. Cook also invented his "light cure" by which ailing members of the crew were exposed to the heat and light of open fires for several hours a day. As a result of this regime of firelight and fresh meat, the crew began to recover. By these means Cook demonstrated the leadership that Amundsen and others so admired in him.[26]

With the return of the sun, spirits rose and health generally improved. During the winter, while locked in the ice pack, the *Belgica* had drifted with the ice from roughly 81° W to 101° W along the seventieth parallel. The ship was still trapped, however, and as the summer progressed, hope diminished that it would be freed. Although openings of water appeared, the steamer found no ice-free path. When attempts to use explosives to break up the ice proved futile, Cook suggested that the crew use huge saws to cut avenues. A channel was chiseled, but the shifting floes closed it again. Finally, on 14 February 1899, the pack broke up enough to free the vessel. After negotiating the oft-blocked routes leading north, the *Belgica* escaped the ice pack on 14 March, setting a course for Punta Arenas, where it arrived two weeks later. The ship reached Antwerp on 5 November.[27]

The *Belgica* was the first expedition to winter inside the Antarctic Circle. Among the scientific results were bathymetric discoveries that included a basin on the south side of the Andes and a continental plateau on the ocean bottom west of Alexander Land. The meteorological observations recorded weather conditions inside the Antarctic Circle over the course of a year. Magnetic studies, though limited in scope, demonstrated the difficulties of working in the Antarctic and yielded only preliminary results. Geographical discoveries included the Belgica Strait and several of its islands. A portion of the Antarctic coastline was charted. Moreover, observations of the shore provided information about glaciers and rock formations. These significant accomplishments were lauded by the editor of the *Nation:* "The highest praise is due to the *Belgica* party for extracting from such an unfavorable environment all that their opportunities permitted, with persistent courage and endurance."[28]

The Germans also were active in southern waters. While the *Belgica* was out of contact with the world, a German vessel was exploring Antarctic seas. In 1897 the Association of German Naturalists and Physicians proposed that a ship be sent to Antarctic waters to conduct deep-sea research. This project differed from the others in the period from 1891 to 1901 in that it was supported entirely by government money. The German Treasury granted the equivalent of fifteen thousand pounds, and the Hamburg-America Line fitted out the vessel at cost.[29]

The *Valdivia* expedition was directed by a civilian, Professor Carl Chun. The ship, commanded by Captain Adalbert Krech, departed from Hamburg on 1 August 1898, stopped in Britain to allow its scientists to visit the *Challenger* offices to confer with the staff, and arrived in South Africa in November. From there the ship sailed in high latitudes and engaged in deep-sea research, following a path that took it to Bouvet Island, the ice pack off Enderby Land, Iles Kerguelen, the Amsterdam Islands, and on to port in Padang, Sumatra. The research conducted on this voyage demonstrated that the Antarctic Sea was deeper than had previously been thought and added to the existing knowledge of deep-sea life.[30]

Despite the increased attention to Antarctic science, the research lacked an overall plan. Therefore, even as Markham was attempting to raise funds, he suggested a scientific program for the proposed expeditions. Speaking at the Seventh International Geographical Congress at Berlin in 1899, he reminded his audience that the opportunities for Antarctic exploration were vast, as previously there had been only one fully equipped expedition, that of James Clark Ross in 1839–43. Sir Clements proposed to divide the Antarctic into four quadrants. Not surprisingly, they were named for Queen Victoria and three British explorers: Ross, Enderby, and Weddell. Markham outlined the work that needed to be undertaken in each section.[31]

Following the recommendation of the Berlin Geographical Society, Markham suggested dividing the Antarctic into two halves. The Ross and Victoria quadrants would comprise the British region in the Antarctic. The

Ross Quadrant was of interest principally for the Great Ice Barrier (Ross Ice Shelf), and the Victoria Quadrant included Victoria Land, explored by Ross, in which the British *Discovery* expedition would concentrate its activities.[32]

Since work in this area would include an assault on the South Magnetic Pole, Sir Clements used this occasion to present his ideas about Antarctic land journeys. He deplored employing dogs in polar travel, arguing that it was a cruel practice and had been proved unworkable. The one successful use of dogs for transport, Markham maintained, was in Peary's crossing of Greenland, an accomplishment achieved only at the expense of the lives of all the animals. Markham added that dogs were useless on ice or broken ground. As neither of these statements was true, Markham reached the incorrect conclusion that men were the only reliable form of polar transport. Citing statistics based on two Arctic man-hauling sledging parties, Markham attempted to show that a group could travel from McMurdo Sound to the South Magnetic Pole and back in three months "without the cruelty of killing a team of dogs by overwork and starvation."[33]

Markham implicitly espoused polar work as a test of manliness. Roland Huntford has perceived this equation of suffering with achievement as an aspect of the English romantic movement. The subsequent disaster at the pole (1911–12), when Robert Falcon Scott and his party died in their attempt to reach 90° South, can be traced to Markham's ideas and his refusal to recognize the benefits of dog transport in polar regions. At the same time that Markham was denigrating the use of dogs, other explorers were convinced of their value. Cook planned on taking dogs for land transport on his Antarctic expedition had he succeeded in launching it. Amundsen was an early convert to the use of dogs. Huntford has cited some of the reasons why dogs are well suited for polar transport: they are efficient in conserving body heat, are sure-footed in snow and ice, eat meat readily available in the Antarctic, and can move heavy loads long distances at far greater speeds over the ice than can other animals. Eventually, British explorers accepted the value of dogs, but not until Scott died at the pole in 1912.[34]

Markham explained the broad scientific goals of the *Discovery* and how they related to society. In addition to the work done aboard ship during the anticipated three summer seasons, a landing party, consisting of an executive officer and a geologist supported by ten men, would conduct sledging activities. As originally proposed, the *Discovery* would take only three civilian scientists, including the surgeon, fewer than the *Southern Cross* carried when it sailed in 1898.[35]

The German portion of the Antarctic, the Weddell and Enderby quadrants, offered many opportunities for science. Larsen, Weddell, and the Scottish whalers had previously plied these waters, and their work posed many questions about the conditions of the ice and land. No one knew whether the Antarctic Peninsula was a series of islands or part of the main body of land. The German party was expected to continue the excellent work done by the *Valdivia* in the Enderby Quadrant. While the British expedition would have its base for magnetic studies at Melbourne, the Germans' would be at Cape Town. In this way both sides of the continent would be observed and the results would give a clearer picture of magnetic phenomena in the South.[36]

Not everyone agreed with Markham's naming of the four sections after British explorers. Edwin S. Balch, a contemporary American historian of the Antarctic, pointed to the achievements of Wilkes and d'Urville, suggesting that they not be slighted.[37]

Nor was Markham's the only general proposal for Antarctic exploration. Arctowski, recently returned from the *Belgica* expedition, suggested a three-pronged approach to Antarctic research. He urged a series of fixed stations to conduct magnetic and meteorological observations between the shore of the continent and the edge of the ice. Moreover, he called for two polar expeditions, each working on a different side of the continent to conduct research simultaneously. Finally, a third ship should be sent to circumnavigate the ice pack and gather data.[38]

Meanwhile, the efforts of the Royal Geographical Society and the Royal Society to launch a British national Antarctic expedition proved disappointing. As 1899 began, less than eight thousand pounds had been added to the five thousand the RGS had originally subscribed. The money came in slowly; small donations of two hundred pounds were more common than large grants, such as Harmsworth's five thousand. Still, Markham remained optimistic. In his address to the Royal Geographical Society in 1899, he reminded his listeners that he and Sherard Osborn had worked twelve years before the 1875 Arctic expedition came to fruition. With this campaign, though, time was more pressing, as other nations threatened to steal Britain's lead. The Belgians were already south, and the Germans were preparing to dispatch an expedition the following year.

"The Antarctic agitation has spread over Europe," and Britain needed to respond.[39]

In March 1899 prospects for the whole project turned around when L. W. Longstaff, a businessman and long-time Fellow of the Royal Geographical Society, asked Markham if twenty-five thousand pounds would launch the project. The president responded enthusiastically. Longstaff, who by his own admission had been "all my life much interested in scientific matters," offered funds for "the advancement of our knowledge of the planet on which we live." Having thus raised forty thousand pounds, Markham was confident that the expedition could sail in 1901 and indicated to Baron Ferdinand von Richthofen, director of the German Antarctic Expedition, that the Germans could count on Britain's cooperation. When Otto Nordenskjöld also announced his intention to journey south in 1901, prospects appeared promising for a great increase in knowledge about Antarctica in the first years of the new century.[40]

Action continued apace. Assured of a successful launch, the Prince of Wales consented to become the patron of the *Discovery* venture, and the duke of York agreed to be named vice-patron. Markham felt that no suitable craft existed in Britain, and on 17 April 1899 he asked Sir William White, a noted naval designer, to recommend an architect to plan a wooden research vessel. White named William Smith, one of the chief contractors for the Admiralty, who had experience with such ships. A committee met in April to develop guidelines for a modern floating research laboratory. The outcome of this group's work, the *Discovery*, was 172 feet long with a beam of 33 feet and a draft of 1,525 tons. The vessel was made of oak covered with greenheart, and the bow was specially reinforced with steel plates. The placement of a magnetic observatory on deck required that no iron or steel be used within 30 feet of this area, and the propeller was designed to be raised to avoid damage in the event of ice. Bids were made, and the project was awarded to the Dundee Ship Building Company, which agreed to construct the vessel for £34,050 plus £9,700 for the engines. Markham named the craft *Discovery*. Like Markham, the Germans ordered a new ship, the *Gauss*, for their expedition (1901–3) under Erich von Drygalski, although the German ship cost substantially less than the *Discovery*.[41]

Despite Longstaff's munificence, additional large donations were not forthcoming, and the subscription campaign stalled. Because the government remained the one great resource, Markham began in early 1899 to maneuver behind the scenes to tap it.

In April he drafted a letter to the Treasury to be sent over the signatures of the presidents of the Royal Society and the Royal Geographical Society, outlining the reasons for an Antarctic expedition and requesting that a deputation be allowed to call on the government. The Joint Antarctic Committee of the Royal Society and the RGS decided that it would be best to delay official contact until the opinion of A. J. Balfour, first lord of the Treasury, could be determined. F. Sidney Parry, private secretary in the Treasury, was asked to ascertain Balfour's mood and to help devise a plan for approaching the government.[42]

Parry advised Sir Clements that the Joint Committee delay contacting the government until the position of Sir Michael Hicks Beach, chancellor of the exchequer, could be ascertained. Parry strongly urged Markham to wait, adding that he would notify Markham when "a fresh step can be taken."[43]

A month passed before Parry gave Markham a favorable report. Knowing that the plea would meet with a positive response, the Royal Society and the RGS then requested that the government receive their deputation.[44]

In June a letter was sent to the prime minister and the first lord of the Treasury seeking a meeting to request public funds for an Antarctic project. The message stated that this cooperation of the Royal Society and the Royal Geographical Society, in combination with other leading British scientific bodies, was unprecedented and that, although more than forty thousand pounds had been subscribed, state support was needed to enable a modest expedition to leave Britain in 1901. Because the Germans had asked the British to cooperate with the *Gauss* venture, it was most pressing that the Imperial Treasury contribute the sixty thousand pounds that was still lacking for even a limited effort.[45]

After the way had been prepared by behind-the-scenes activity, a formal deputation waited on Balfour on 22 June. In a private note to Markham, Parry had urged that the group be as strong and as large as possible and that the press be notified. Noting that "the bigger the splash made, the greater the hope of success," Parry also recommended that the practical aspects of exploration be emphasized, especially the role of magnetism in navigation, and that scientific details be kept to a minimum.[46]

The deputation represented many of the most influential British scientists of the day. Markham opened the meeting by underscoring the need for a Treasury grant. Despite tangible improvements in deep-sea dredging and sounding and the advent of steam for navigation, fifty years had passed since an official British expedition had sailed Antarctic waters. When rebuffed earlier by the government, he explained, the Royal Society and the Royal Geographical Society had taken it on themselves to launch a campaign in which more than forty thousand pounds had been raised. Having shown that there was interest in their effort, the group requested Treasury support.[47]

In the past, said Markham, the government had seen the need for scientific endeavors and had underwritten such efforts, aware that the results of pure science eventually lead to commercial gain. Equally important, the cabinets of Lord Melbourne, Sir Robert Peel, and Lord Beaconsfield, all of which had sent previous expeditions to polar regions, knew that such work was among the best opportunities for training naval personnel. The German project, moreover, had received a grant of sixty thousand pounds from Berlin, which ensured that the vessel sailing from Kiel would be properly equipped. "The honor of our country and the cause of science demand that we be able to cooperate with the Germans in these endeavors."[48]

Other members of the deputation spoke about the scientific benefits to be derived from South Polar research. William Thomson, Lord Kelvin, president of the Royal Society of Edinburgh, told Balfour that "surely as Britannia rules the waves, it is of primary importance for England to take part in the exploration of her own realm." Kelvin argued that the need to understand the movement of ice in southern waters was essential for the safety of ships plying that part of the globe. At the time, many vessels had to detour around areas where icebergs were suspected because ships lacked sufficient information to sail safely in those waters. The most important result of the *Challenger* venture had been an indication of how little was known about southern seas.[49]

The advocate arguing from the strongest position was Professor A. W. Rucker, who spoke on the need to increase knowledge of terrestrial magnetism. Rucker had recently served as president of the International Conference on Terrestrial Magnetism, a body that included representatives from across Europe and the United States. He explained that terrestrial magnetism was among the most pressing scientific issues of the day. This was an especially opportune moment to send forth an expedition, he felt, since cooperation with the Germans would yield more significant results than any single effort or any two programs operating in different years. Rucker also foresaw the need for a specially constructed wooden vessel to undertake this research.[50]

Although Balfour did not claim to understand the details of the scientific questions this expedition hoped to answer, he agreed that the government needed to consider the proposition seriously. He was not dissuaded by the emphasis on pure science as opposed to commercial possibilities.

> I take a different view—a view based upon the scientific experience of the past. If our predecessors in the last two centuries had taken any narrow utilitarian view of their work, it is manifest that our ignorance of the planet on which we live would be much more profound than it is at present; and it would not be creditable to an age which, above all other ages, flatters itself that it is scientific, if we were without reluctance to acquiesce in the total ignorance which now envelops us with regard to so enormous a portion of the southern hemisphere of our planet.[51]

Moreover, he was particularly pleased to hear of the proposed cooperation with the German scientific community, seeing a coordinated effort as another opportunity to promote the international character of pure science. Regarding conflict in the Antarctic, Balfour added, "There cannot be any territorial rivalry between any of the countries engaged in Antarctic exploration; and that such rivalry as there may be, must be of a purely scientific character."[52]

Success was soon in Markham's grasp. The years of petitioning came to an end on 3 July 1899 when the government offered the Royal Society and the Royal Geographical Society forty-five thousand pounds for the Antarctic expedition on the condition that the money be matched by private subscriptions.[53] Murray believed that the funds were given more as a response to the assistance of foreign powers for their own national expeditions than as a farsighted commitment to Britain's adventurers. Even though only three thousand pounds of matching monies was lacking, that amount was not easily found. Markham appealed to possible donors, but the response was disappointing. Harmsworth would contribute no more.[54] In the absence of other subscribers, Markham cajoled the Royal

Geographical Society into donating the money. Thus the RGS contributed eight thousand pounds, an extraordinarily large amount given the society's limited resources.

F. Sidney Parry, who had helped prepare the way for the deputation to Balfour, also assisted Markham to secure the naval officers that Goschen had previously denied. Parry suggested that Markham ask the sea lords for their support, as their advice would be influential. In the end this strategy worked.[55]

While unable to amass all that he had hoped for, Markham finally had enough money to send his expedition south. Even ninety thousand pounds was less than he had campaigned for, and a much smaller amount than the one hundred fifty thousand pounds that Murray thought essential to send two ships to Antarctica for three summers and two winters. Murray warned that limited funds meant that certain interests had to be eliminated. The alternatives, he suggested, would be for the British Association for the Advancement of Science to contribute fifty thousand pounds toward the effort, or to find two additional donors as generous as Longstaff.[56]

Markham had gambled all along that government support would be forthcoming, and he was correct. His years of toil had resulted in the funding of a great national Antarctic expedition. Before it sailed, though, another group of explorers left England to become the first persons to winter on the Antarctic continent.

SIX

The Interloper

Sir Clements Markham's plans to launch the first entirely scientific British Antarctic expedition were dashed by Carsten E. Borchgrevink. From the moment the *Antarctic* docked at Melbourne in March 1895, Borchgrevink was determined to return to Antarctica at the head of his own expedition. Although he was less qualified to lead than others, Borchgrevink was the first to sail. Even though his adventure was a forerunner of the great national Antarctic undertaking of 1901, the efforts of Borchgrevink and his companions have been largely ignored by historians.

Borchgrevink left England in 1896 for Australia to seek capital for his venture. There he met Louis Bernacchi (1876–1942), a young scientist working at the Melbourne Observatory. Impressed with Bernacchi, Borchgrevink asked him to join his staff.[1] Failing to find money in Australia, Borchgrevink returned to England to secure a sponsor. Within weeks he had found publisher George Newnes (1851–1910).

Newnes, the son of a Congregational minister, had been educated at Silcoate and the City of London School, where he was a contemporary of Herbert H. Asquith. On leaving school Newnes was apprenticed without pay for five years to a firm in the City, where his exceptional ability with figures brought him to the attention of his superiors. He once wagered that he could do the business's year-end accounting in twelve hours rather than in the ten days spent by the bookkeeping department.

He won the bet and was given a promotion, whereupon he brashly asked for the hundred-pound salary the position normally paid. His employer first refused, then relented.[2]

Newnes left that position to start a publishing venture. The 1870 Education Act had helped create a literate public that wanted to read nonintellectually demanding materials. Dissatisfied with contemporary periodicals, Newnes decided that a market existed for a morally uplifting magazine, light in tone and lively in style. Having no money, he appealed to several wealthy persons for the funds to launch his dream but was rebuffed at every turn. Finally, he raised the capital by establishing a successful vegetarian restaurant. Within a few weeks he sold it for enough money to provide the funds for his project.[3]

Newnes published the first *Tit-Bits* on 30 October 1881. It was an immediate triumph, selling five thousand copies in two hours in Manchester alone. Within weeks, and for the next thirty years, *Tit-Bits* was one of the most successful periodicals in Britain. Newnes's good fortune was founded on two concepts: articles that held the attention of the reader and schemes that promoted the periodical. Among his marketing ploys was an offer of a hundred pounds to anyone who had been reading *Tit-Bits* for a given period of time. A woman who claimed that her husband would have qualified had he not been killed in a train wreck was awarded the prize when a copy of *Tit-Bits* was found on his body. Subsequently, Newnes instituted in every issue of *Tit-Bits* a life insurance policy of a hundred pounds for anyone killed in a train wreck while reading the magazine.[4]

Newnes's achievement prompted imitation; at one point twenty-two similar magazines were in print. Only one mounted a serious challenge: *Answers to Correspondents*, founded by Alfred C. Harmsworth, an early contributor to *Tit-Bits* (and a subsequent financial donor to the *Discovery* expedition). Harmsworth's accomplishment created a rivalry between the two most successful popular press publishers of the day.[5]

Newnes expanded his empire. After *Tit-Bits* his best-selling effort was *The Strand Magazine*, which had the good fortune to carry most of the Sherlock Holmes stories. Despite great commercial success, Newnes always remained open to new ideas and projects. He never refused an appointment to anyone who claimed to call on an issue of great importance, a trait that Borchgrevink used to advantage.[6]

Borchgrevink and Newnes became acquainted as a result of an article on the *Antarctic* forays which Borchgrevink wrote for *The Strand Magazine*.

Newnes had a history of supporting projects that caught his attention, and his publishing experience made him aware of the publicity value of exploration. Harmsworth, his principal rival, also backed such ventures and had assisted Lieutenant Robert Peary in his North Pole explorations. In addition, Harmsworth underwrote Jackson's journey to Franz Josef Land, and this generosity won him wide praise. Such expeditions, Newnes knew, made good copy, and Harmsworth had demonstrated that exclusive reports of these undertakings sold papers. Newnes had been a brash young man once and appreciated the quality in others; science and commerce could be combined. By maintaining exclusive rights to publication after the adventure, he hoped to recover the costs.[7]

Borchgrevink's enthusiasm, determination, and experience aboard the *Antarctic* persuaded Newnes to underwrite the endeavor. Newnes agreed to provide forty thousand pounds to outfit the *Southern Cross* expedition. This sum was more than Markham had raised in two years and was sufficient to cover all Borchgrevink's expenses.[8]

Despite the criticism later heaped on Borchgrevink for his lack of ability, his preparations for the expedition were remarkably thorough. With his financial problems solved, he began making arrangements for the voyage. He traveled to Norway to purchase his ship, the *Pollux*, which he rechristened *Southern Cross*. A sturdy, barque-rigged whaler, it boasted a bow of eleven feet of oak and sides measuring at least three feet thick. It was constructed by Colin Archer, the designer and builder of the *Fram*. Refitted in Norway, it sailed to England in the summer of 1898.[9]

Although the *Southern Cross* expedition was a much smaller enterprise than the one envisioned for the *Discovery*, Borchgrevink planned a larger scientific staff. In selecting his crew he chose men he thought would work well together and be sufficiently versatile to handle several responsibilities. Borchgrevink wanted his scientists to collect data that would be analyzed by experts after his return to England.[10]

To captain the *Southern Cross* Borchgrevink selected someone he knew from his *Antarctic* days, the experienced ice master Bernhard Jensen, whom Borchgrevink described as having "eagle eyes, a man he looked and a man he was." Jorgen Peterson was chosen first mate. The other responsible ship's officers were also Norwegians, as were most of the seamen. All had experience with ice conditions in the Arctic.[11]

In the selection of the scientific staff Borchgrevink was singularly wise. Louis Bernacchi was invited to join, based on the favorable impression he had made on Borchgrevink in Australia. Although only twenty-two, he had three years' experience working with magnetism and meteorological studies. He was a keen observer and a well-trained scientist. His attempt to join the *Belgica* had demonstrated an interest in polar matters, and he subsequently became an important figure in Antarctic circles, serving with Scott on the *Discovery*.[12]

William Colbeck (1871–1930), a capable sailor and navigator with a decade of service in merchant ships, became the expedition's magnetic observer and cartographer. To prepare for his work on the *Southern Cross* he studied magnetism at Kew Observatory. The highly respected Nikolai Hanson (1870–99) was named zoologist. Trained at the University of Christiana under Robert Collett and recommended by him, Hanson was working at the British Museum at the time of his appointment. His efforts in the Norwegian Arctic had been praised by Robert Bowdler-Sharpe, head of the British Museum's Natural History Division. A fellow Norwegian was also selected as medical officer: Herlof Klovstad (1868–1900), who had been educated at the University of Christiana and at age thirty was older than all the men but Borchgrevink.[13]

Two others completed the staff. Anton Fougner (1870–1932), who signed on as a general handyman but became a scientific assistant, was acknowledged as the crew's best skier. Hugh Blackwell Evans (1874–1975) was a young Englishman who had lived in Canada's Northwest Territories. Newnes became acquainted with Evans's family from the publisher's Arctic whaling activities and recommended Evans as assistant zoologist.[14]

Rounding out the crew were two Lapps, Ole Must (1877–1934) and Persen Savio (1877–1905). Their selection was one of Borchgrevink's cleverest ideas. These two men, originally chosen for their expertise with the dogs, proved to be valuable members of the group. Their lifelong experience in harsh Arctic conditions provided the neophytes with a wealth of practical skills. The experiment of taking Lapps was not repeated in the Heroic Era, thus squandering one of the valuable lessons Borchgrevink's expedition provided.

Each of the staff signed an agreement with Borchgrevink giving him certain publication rights regarding the expedition. This document, clearly spelling out the responsibilities on both sides, was later to be the cause of some discontent on the part of the scientists. Still, the use of a written agreement was an improvement over Gerlache's approach on the *Belgica*. On that adventure Arctowski had criticized the commander for the absence of such a contract, although the lack of one made it possible for Arctowski to publish his research from the voyage.[15]

Borchgrevink made careful preparations for supplies and equipment. Unlike some explorers of the Heroic Era, he recognized from the outset the value of dogs and became the first to use them in the Antarctic. Samoyeds were procured after an eight-hundred-mile journey across northern Siberia by Russell Jeaffreson, Borchgrevink's agent. The dogs proved their worth in the extreme conditions on this venture. Borchgrevink was also a consistent advocate of skiing. All the Norwegians were acquainted with this form of travel, and eventually the English members of the *Southern Cross* became proficient. Though not the first to use skis in the Antarctic (Larsen's crew used them on the *Jason* expedition), Borchgrevink's men proved the folly of working in the South Polar regions without an appreciation of skis.

Borchgrevink also provided the *Southern Cross* with kayaks—light, wood-framed, canvas-covered craft, widely used in Norway and ideal for maneuvering in and around icy waters. They proved very useful on the trip. Unknown to Borchgrevink at the time, the *Belgica* crew later noted its own lack of these versatile boats. Although Borchgrevink considered using a balloon for observations, an idea first put forth by Sir Joseph Hooker, none was taken.[16]

Overall, the *Southern Cross* was a well-equipped endeavor. The scientific instruments were first-rate, but the scientists would later rue not having duplicates of some equipment. Particular attention was paid to the choice of a variety of well-made tinned food. Although the experiences of the *Belgica* were not known to Borchgrevink, he was aware of the danger of scurvy, a disease some attributed to incorrectly preserved foods. Because of the care that went into the selection of foodstuffs and equipment, the men experienced no serious problems from these vital life supports. This good fortune was not shared by subsequent expeditions, an indication of the quality of supplies Borchgrevink chose.[17]

In defining the goals of the *Southern Cross*, Borchgrevink aimed for a limited set of achievable results. First, he wanted to prove that humans could endure an Antarctic winter. Second, he planned to procure as complete a set of meteorological and magnetic observations as possible, thereby giving scientists an entire year's data to study. In addition, he hoped to locate and if possible reach the South Magnetic Pole. Borchgrevink also anticipated finding new species of flora and fauna, making careful investigations of South Victoria Land, and charting new territory. Absent from his goals was a trip to the South Geographic Pole, in 1898 not yet the object of desire that it became within a decade. Also missing was a definite plan for commercial gain, although both Newnes and Borchgrevink hoped for some financial success to crown the scientific achievements.[18]

Borchgrevink's triumph in the face of Markham's attempt to launch the national enterprise evoked mixed reactions. Publicly, most people associated with Antarctic exploration wished Borchgrevink well. Even Sir Clements in his presidential address in 1897 hoped Borchgrevink would find "all possible success." Privately, it was another matter. Markham was livid at Borchgrevink's success in raising the forty thousand pounds that Markham believed should have gone to his own undertaking. That sum, added to what had already been raised, would have ensured the complete program of the *Discovery* expedition, including a second ship. That Borchgrevink was not one of the inner circle of British science was annoying enough, but he was not even British. Even in public Markham complained that Borchgrevink was Norwegian. Actually, Borchgrevink referred to himself as a British colonial who had emigrated to Australia; he was half-British by virtue of his English mother.[19]

Markham wrote a scathing confidential letter to H. R. Mill excoriating Borchgrevink. Sir Clements averred that the Norwegian had paid far too much for the *Pollux* and suggested that it cost less than the stated price, implying that Borchgrevink had pocketed the difference. The president charged that the *Pollux* was unsound and that Borchgrevink had gone to great lengths to hide this from Newnes, even to the point of providing a certificate of seaworthiness that Markham believed was a forgery. The reason for refitting the boat in Norway was not that a strike prevented the work from being done in England, as Borchgrevink had asserted, but to cover the sorry state of the vessel before and after refitting. That Borchgrevink did not have the barque classed at Lloyd's, something not required because the *Southern Cross* sailed as a yacht, was cited by Markham as further proof of Borchgrevink's duplicity. Markham described him as impudent and stupid but cunning and unprincipled.[20]

Markham attacked Newnes for choosing a Norwegian when so many British commanders were prepared and able to command. The president reported to Mill that the Norwegian newspapers were making light of Borchgrevink's "British" expedition, noting that with a Norwegian ship, commander, and crew, the only British involvement was the funding, much of which was being spent in Norway. Finally, Markham asserted, the dogs Borchgrevink bought were not from Siberia but from Archangel and were "unsuitable and untrained."[21] Markham's criticism of the vessel appears unwarranted, given the success of the voyage. Mill apparently did not respond. Markham made it clear that Borchgrevink was persona non grata as far as the RGS was concerned.

Despite Markham's disapproval, preparations were completed in August 1898. On the eve of departure Newnes hosted a farewell luncheon. It was a terribly hot day, a stark contrast to the cold that awaited the explorers. Neither Markham nor any RGS officers appeared in an official capacity, although two of the society's members risked the wrath of Sir Clements by taking part. Sir Erasmus Ommanney attended, as did H. R. Mill, who proposed a toast to the expedition's success. Markham later reproached Mill for attending. Newnes spoke briefly about his hopes for the venture, thanking all who had assisted in the project and noting that the RGS had shown great courtesy toward the undertaking. Regarding the suggestion put forth by Markham that the *Southern Cross* should alter its plans to search for the overdue *Belgica*, Newnes said that Gerlache knew of Borchgrevink's route and therefore it was best to keep to the original program because the Belgian might attempt to reconnoiter with the *Southern Cross*.[22] Finally, on 22 August 1898, the barque slipped from St. Katherine's Dock, stopping to coal at Gravesend, where thousands were at the quays to wish the adventurers bon voyage.

As the *Southern Cross* proceeded directly to Madeira, the voyage allowed the men to settle into life aboard ship. The samoyeds were a constant problem because they suffered from the heat; canvas awnings were kept wet to help cool the animals. The stench on deck caused by the dogs produced considerable discomfort for the crew, but they and the animals soon adapted. All the dogs were named, and often a particular dog became the favorite of one of the crew.[23]

At Madeira the scientists investigated the island while supplies were taken aboard. Their late return to the steamer prompted a nasty response from Borchgrevink that angered the scientists. It was the first indication of the friction that marred relations between the scientific staff and the commander.[24]

From Madeira the ship proceeded to St. Cruz and St. Vincent, where several men became ill with an undetermined tropical ailment. Although all appeared to recover, it proved to be the beginning of a series of health problems that eventually led to Hanson's death.[25]

Ninety-eight days out of London, the *Southern Cross* reached Tasmania, steaming into Adventure Bay on 28 November, Borchgrevink having decided to omit the Cape Town stop because of a storm. The following day the ship proceeded to Hobart, where the crew received a warm welcome. It was a homecoming for Bernacchi and a fortnight of celebration and preparation for all. The men were feted by various groups throughout their stay, the grandest occasion being the program on the 2d of December hosted by the Royal Society of Tasmania. Formally attired guests were ushered through a doorway guarded on each side by a Lapp in national costume. Exhibits of polar equipment were on display, and speeches welcomed the explorers to Tasmania. Letters of congratulations were read from those unable to attend. One message was from J. W. Agnew, one of the oldest members of the society, who had been present to wish Ross success in 1840 and regretted that illness prevented him from toasting Borchgrevink as well. After the opening remarks Borchgrevink spoke of the expedition, stressing its scientific nature, although he evoked a humorous response when he commented that if they found a gold nugget they would take note of it. Bernacchi closed the evening by thanking the Tasmanians for their kindness.[26]

The *Southern Cross* sailed from Adventure Bay on 19 December with an uncertain future. So little was known of the southern regions that not even one direct winter temperature reading had been made within the Antarctic Circle. On departing from Tasmania, the crew lost all communication with the world. The vessel took carrier pigeons, several of which were set free, but none reached its destination and at least one returned to the ship so exhausted that it died shortly thereafter. Until the men returned to Australia, they would depend on their own resources, their lives protected only by the timber of the *Southern Cross*. The degree of danger was reinforced by the knowledge that the only ship engaged in similar work, the *Belgica*, was overdue and presumed lost with all hands. Before the explorers lay the "land of unsurpassed desolation."[27]

Little hint of ice appeared until the men suddenly found themselves entering the ice pack on 30 December at 158° E, farther east than the route Ross and Wilkes had shown to be ideal. Colbeck unsuccessfully urged that they enter the ice further west. Immediately, the fauna changed; gone was the sooty albatross, replaced by visits from white ice petrels. Penguins and seals also appeared, affording the scientists their first opportunity to secure specimens. Hanson eagerly approached his first seal and drove an ice pick into its skull. Rather than killing the animal, the attack merely angered it. The seal charged Hanson, who sought refuge by jumping on its back. That perch proved equally dangerous, but several sailors killed the animal.[28]

The men used their slow passage through the ice to disembark from the ship occasionally. The English learned to ski, while the Norwegians sharpened their skills. Fougner even demonstrated downhill skiing, using an eroded iceberg as a slope. The recreation hours were not without danger. At one point Borchgrevink failed to stop at the edge of a floe and continued into the frigid water. The long Norwegian skis floated to the surface, keeping Borchgrevink's head underwater, but Fougner ended this inglorious episode with a timely rescue. The men also lost one of their favorite dogs when it apparently fell into a waterhole at night.[29]

The ice was a stunning sight. Huge tabular icebergs averaging 120 feet high and ranging to several miles in length formed a dangerous maze through which the *Southern Cross* maneuvered. Days of wonder turned into weeks of concern as the ship became imprisoned in the ice pack. The eastern entrance to the floes had taken the explorers into the middle of the pack. Oceanographic studies show that the *Southern Cross* had chosen a path through the heaviest part of the ice pack. In late January the ship was temporarily pinned among the ice floes. As the pressure built up, the barque was lifted four feet and held there by the grip of the ice. Eventually, a storm freed the ship, but the crew feared the horrors of being frozen in and forced to winter away from all shelter and food, other than the supplies on board for Borchgrevink's party. In one week the *Southern Cross* moved only thirty miles closer to the Antarctic coast, a rate that threatened hopes of landing in South Victoria Land.[30]

Borchgrevink and Jenson alternated in the crow's nest as they attempted to guide the craft toward open seas, taking advantage of the ice blink, a polar phenomenon by which refracted light at the horizon shows whether there is ice beyond the field of vision. Open water is indicated by dark vapor clouds in the sky at the horizon, a condition called a water sky. On deck it was bitterly cold. The crew either had to climb the rigging wearing mittens, which froze to the lines and were ripped from their hands, or had to go barehanded in the ropes for brief periods before their hands became numb and useless.[31]

Not all the cold was above deck. An incident occurred below that chilled the relationship between the scientists and their commander. Before landing at Hobart, Borchgrevink had ordered that no letters be mailed from Tasmania. When the scientists protested, Borchgrevink reconsidered. Apparently, he had acted in good faith by attempting to safeguard the investment of his patron, who wanted to profit from the exclusive publication of any information about the expedition. Letters home threatened that monopoly, as such messages often were released to local newspapers. While they passed through the ice pack, Borchgrevink wrote a second order, this time forbidding mail to return with the *Southern Cross* from Cape Adare to Australia. Again the scientists objected and Borchgrevink relented. Although he rescinded both commands, the damage had already been done by creating a lingering distrust in the scientific crew which, in the long winter months of confinement, grew into animosity.[32]

A further incident exacerbated the differences. Colbeck had argued with Borchgrevink over the route through the ice, and in early February the issue came up again. Borchgrevink then decreed that Colbeck could not winter at Cape Adare as planned but instead would be sent back to Australia with the ship. The rift was smoothed over, and in the end Colbeck was allowed to remain with the shore party, but the event reinforced the staff's belief that the commander's actions were arbitrary.[33]

The decision to enter the ice pack so far to the west further undermined the scientists' view of their leader. The lengthy stay in the ice threatened the possibility of making a landfall or of attempting to search for sites other than Cape Adare. Borchgrevink also lost stature in the eyes of his scientists, who were cautious and skeptical observers, when he claimed to discover new land that was later proven to be one of the Balleny Islands.[34]

On 9 February 1899, when a severe storm racked the vessel, the captain turned the steamer north and east for protection. Guided by a water sky, Jensen brought the *Southern Cross* to an open channel outside the ice pack. The vessel was now roughly in the same geographical position it had been in six weeks earlier. Jensen sailed southeast to reach a more advantageous point to reenter the pack. On 14 February the *Southern Cross* entered the ice further west; this proved successful. Because of the lateness of the season, the floes were more broken in that area and the barque pushed through the ice into open water in under six hours.[35]

With open seas ahead, a course was set for Cape Adare. Its dark rock, which was sighted on the evening of 15 February, stood out in contrast to the world of white. The small, low-lying, uninviting beach, difficult to detect at first, did not inspire confidence as a wintering place. A storm prevented a landing for thirty-six hours.[36]

As midnight approached on the 17th, Borchgrevink, Bernacchi, and Savio rowed ashore. On landing, Bernacchi congratulated Borchgrevink. The brief foray showed the commander that the beach was much as it had been four years earlier; Robertson Bay was for the moment free of ice. Returning to the Southern Cross, Borchgrevink and his men prepared to land supplies, a task that had to be accomplished quickly because of the lateness of the season. Although Borchgrevink had briefly considered wintering the Southern Cross at Cape Adare, he kept to his original plan of having the ship return to the safety of Australia. It was too dangerous to risk the men's only lifeline in totally unknown ice conditions.[37]

Borchgrevink's reasons for choosing Cape Adare apparently stemmed from the impression he had gathered in 1895 that the peninsula was partially protected from harsh winds and enjoyed more moderate temperatures than other areas. He believed that the presence of penguins meant a hospitable location, though that assumption shows more his lack of knowledge of those birds than his understanding of meteorology. Ross had tried to land at Cape Adare, but his approach was blocked by eight miles of pack ice. Borchgrevink's choice of the cape was made primarily because it was a locale he had seen. It was also the one place he had mentioned in his efforts to raise capital for the expedition. Unfortunately, the cape did not prove a good choice, and the site handicapped the scientists in their attempts to gather useful data. Had the Southern Cross cleared the ice pack more quickly, the base of operations might have been established further south in a more favorable place such as McMurdo Sound or Wood Bay, resulting in more and better opportunities for exploration and research.[38]

Unloading took twelve days. The Southern Cross was maneuvered as close to land as possible, and the dogs were brought ashore first. They promptly killed dozens of penguins. Supplies were transported to shore in whaleboats; from there the process often required wading with the boxes through the frigid water.[39]

The work took longer than expected because of bad weather. Storms arose quickly, and on the night of the 21st the five scientists and two Lapps were caught on land when a gale came up. Fortunately, the Lapps had a tent with them and the seven men managed to survive the night, aided by many of the dogs, which crawled inside and slept on top of

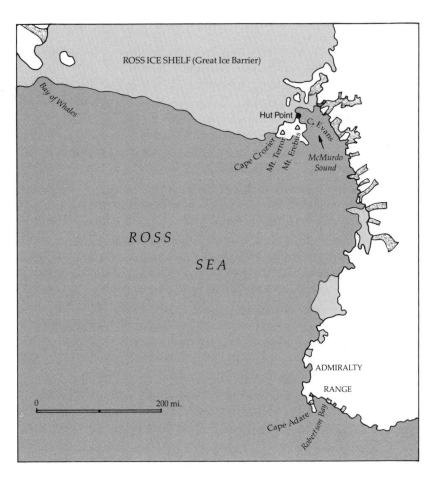

Map 3
Cape Adare

the men. On board ship the storm wreaked havoc—the anchor was torn loose, and the barque was driven toward the rocks by fierce winds. Only by steaming full speed ahead was the *Southern Cross* able to keep from being blown on the shoals. During the night Borchgrevink considered cutting away the main mast, but that proved impossible in the torrent of ice and stones that rained down on the deck. The vessel survived. Two nights later a less severe tempest battered the ship.[40]

Onshore the men began assembling the two prefabricated huts, which were composed of numbered sections for easy assembly. One building was used for living quarters, the other for provisions and equipment. The structures, well designed and sturdy, were erected four yards apart; the space between them was protected from the elements and was used for storage. This area also allowed for easy passage between the two huts during inclement weather. The floors and walls were double-layered, with papier-mâché between the inner and outer timbers for insulation. Doors opened inward to allow the men to dig themselves out of a snowdrift.[41]

The simple dwelling, fifteen feet on each side, housed ten men for almost a year. Borchgrevink followed the example of whaling ships in making each bunk an enclosed cubicle into which a person could retreat for some measure of privacy. In these coffinlike enclosures the men slept, wrote, and read.[42]

By the beginning of March the provisions had been landed. On 1 March, Borchgrevink hoisted the Union Jack given to the expedition by the duke of York; the party gathered around the flagpole while the commander made a short speech. After the ceremony the men repaired to the steamer to prepare for its departure, which could not be significantly delayed, as pack ice was forming in the bay. There the crew and the wintering party said a final good-bye. On returning to the cape those on shore fired a farewell volley from their rifles.[43]

On the evening of 1 March the *Southern Cross* turned north, leaving behind ten men to attempt what had never been done before: to winter on the Antarctic continent. As the barque sailed from view, the men knew that if the vessel was lost, they would be marooned; no plans existed for a relief expedition. Ole Must was particularly moved by the departure of the *Southern Cross* and followed it along the shore as far as he could until the ship disappeared below the horizon.[44]

SEVEN

Pilgrims on the Ice

The day after the *Southern Cross* sailed, Robertson Bay froze over. If the ship had been delayed, it would have been trapped by the ice and perhaps crushed by ice pressures during the winter. The men would have been marooned.

The members of the land party spent their first days bringing the remaining supplies from shore to the base, which Borchgrevink had named Camp Ridley in honor of his mother. Alcohol and other liquids that required some protection from the cold were stored in the loft over the living quarters. The crew killed as many Weddell seals as could be found to provide the dogs with fresh meat, and the skins were added to the insulation in the roofs of the buildings. The Lapps used the animals' fur to make warm clothing and shoes. Sealskin boots stuffed with sennegras, a dried plant that provided excellent protection from cold and damp, became the footwear of choice during the expedition.[1]

While the staff continued to set up camp, Borchgrevink and Bernacchi climbed Cape Adare on 12 March to a height of 3,600 feet. This first sojourn exposed one of the main drawbacks of the location. The trek was a steep and difficult climb, and at the top the view to the south revealed that no easy route existed toward the mountains of South Victoria. The two men returned to Camp Ridley to help transport the last of the provisions to the huts and to store them for the winter.[2]

While Newnes's birthday on the 13th provided a brief diversion, of more interest to the scientists was the first appearance of the aurora australis two days later. Though it was not as brilliant as later displays, the men were struck by the awesome beauty of nature's light show. As winter progressed, the aurora took on a different meaning, for these spectacular phenomena preceded violent storms.[3]

The first sighting of the southern lights prompted an altercation between Bernacchi and Borchgrevink. The commander wanted to use the large telescope to view the aurora, but Bernacchi argued that nothing would be visible through the instrument. Borchgrevink chided his young scientist, saying that he had observed the northern lights that way many times. When the device was set up, Bernacchi proved to be correct. Although Borchgrevink apologized, it did not ease the tension when he added, "Bernacchi's always right," a comment that the young Tasmanian took as a snide remark. To Bernacchi the incident was further proof of his commander's incompetence in scientific matters.[4]

Barely having taken time to organize the headquarters, Borchgrevink prepared to embark on the first sledging effort of the fall: an exploration of the inner part of Robertson Bay. Before he left the base, taking Fougner and Colbeck, Borchgrevink gave Bernacchi a letter outlining rescue procedures should the group become overdue and named Bernacchi his successor should he fail to return.[5]

Instead of being away ten days as planned, Borchgrevink's party returned within forty-eight hours. Despite the assistance of a second band of men in hauling provisions part way toward their destination, the effort to proceed southward was hampered by rugged terrain. Moreover, the sledging crew met with terrible weather, which caused Borchgrevink to retreat prematurely to Camp Ridley. The small second group that helped the sledgers get under way nearly met with a fatal accident while returning to the encampment. Evans slipped on an outcropping of solid ice and was tumbling to a certain death on the jagged rocks below when Hanson pulled him to safety.[6]

The same storm that forestalled Borchgrevink struck the base camp. Winds of eighty miles per hour drove several dog kennels out to sea. One of the two large boats was destroyed when it was blown away, and the men were able to preserve the second vessel only by lashing it down and filling it with coal for ballast. The violent gale caused the men at Ridley to fear for the safety of their colleagues, but Borchgrevink's party returned to camp the next day.[7]

As the end of March approached, the group felt even more isolated when the penguins, seals, and skuas, anticipating winter, left the cape. Temperatures dropped noticeably, and the days grew shorter. The scientific work continued, though, as Colbeck and Bernacchi established the magnetic observatory in one of the Lapp tents some distance from the huts. Without heat, this location was painfully cold for the observers. Measurements were taken every two hours from nine in the morning until nine at night. These records became one of the most important achievements of the expedition.[8]

The harsh weather lasted through the remainder of March and into April. Although the climatic conditions at Cape Adare proved a problem for the men throughout the year, the scientists proceeded with their work. In April, soundings were begun in the bay. Hanson embarked on fishing forays that yielded new species and an important supplement to the larder.[9]

Before the onset of winter a second attempt was made to explore the southern reaches of Robertson Bay. On 22 April, Borchgrevink departed with Fougner, Bernacchi, and Savio, taking provisions for a twenty-day sojourn. Setting out over the frozen bay, the company was halted in late afternoon by patches of thin ice. A bivouac was selected at the shore. With difficulty the men found a small beach that appeared to afford a secure sleeping area, but a storm arose overnight, breaking up the ice in the bay. The waves of the open sea rolled over their tents, forcing the campers to higher ground and swamping their position. A small ledge above the high-tide mark gave them a precarious perch on which to ride out the tempest, which lasted through the next day. By the time the storm ended on the third day, the sledgers were cut off from Camp Ridley: above them were perpendicular cliffs, below them the open sea.[10]

To extricate the group from this situation, Fougner offered to take the kayak and return to Cape Adare for help, but Borchgrevink refused. Five hours later the commander reconsidered and sent Fougner and Savio off in the tiny craft. Taking only a small packet of provisions, the two departed at dark. They had been gone only a short time before the remaining men noticed a strange silence. The sound of the waves on the shore below had ceased—the bay was full of slush ice the consistency of thick porridge. This sudden change caught the men by surprise, and their thoughts dwelled on Fougner and Savio in a canvas boat that could easily be punctured by the loose pack.[11]

The men passed another twenty-four hours on the ledge, during which time they made an unsuccessful attempt to find a way out by cutting steps in the snow to form a path to the crest of the mountain. The next day, 26 April, brought a surprise. Fougner and Savio returned from the north via the ice slope above the ledge. Relieved to discover the two had survived, Borchgrevink and the others learned how the two explorers had been forced to put into shore when the kayak was threatened by the ice. The skill of the Lapp proved valuable again. After landing, the two men had killed a seal and, using the blubber for fuel, cooked a steak dinner. The following day Savio and Fougner had doubled back overland, carving steps up the steep slope, and returned to Borchgrevink's group a day later.[12]

The reassembled party was prevented from moving during a storm on the 27th. The next day the entire company retraced the steps of Fougner and Savio and followed the route via the ridge that separated them from Camp Ridley. The travelers continued over the mountain, struggling through the night to reach Cape Adare. It was an exciting experience that showed the men that the Antarctic left no latitude for error.[13]

The sun's path grew steadily lower in the sky and disappeared on 15 May. The men were as moved by the setting of the sun as they had been by the departure of the fauna. Bernacchi captured his colleagues' feelings:

> We watched the departing sun as it slowly skimmed along the horizon like a tired traveler after a long weary march; and yet it seemed reluctant to leave us and to depart with a certain amount of regret, for even after it had dropped below the horizon a deep red afterglow remained in the sky, and a lurid crimson flush lingered caressingly on the distant snowpeaks for some hours afterwards.[14]

Winter in the Antarctic is a trying time. The crew of the *Belgica* fared badly; one member went insane, and nearly all the others suffered emotional problems. The personnel of the *Southern Cross* escaped such trauma, but their winter was not without emotional stress.

Scientific work provided the staff with useful and interesting activity during the long nights. Despite the difficulties, the scientists performed admirably, maintaining regular meteorological notations and magnetic observations. Throughout the dark months the team gathered and preserved specimens for later study in England. Photography was included as part of the scientific program, for few photographs of the Antarctic were extant before the *Southern Cross* sailed. Bernacchi was the principal photographer, even though Evans also had a camera and shared in the chores. Although the staff had excellent equipment to develop negatives, photographic work in the hut took great patience and involved considerable hardship. Snow and ice had to be melted to provide water for the solutions, and to ensure complete darkness, the work had to be done after the others had retired. The chemicals froze unless great care was taken. Developing the film meant preparing gelatin negatives and then mounting these membranes between two sheets of glass. These efforts eventually paid dividends to those in England who studied the great white South. Bernacchi also had an early movie camera and made several cinemagraphs during the year.[15]

Throughout the winter the staff lived in close quarters with surprisingly little divisiveness. The hut was tiny, but the enclosed bunks gave a measure of privacy that moderated the effects of being locked up together through the long darkness. In bad weather the confinement was felt keenly. During a storm, white-out conditions existed outside; snow driven by the wind made it impossible to see a foot in front of one's face. Leaving the shelter for any reason required roping up to prevent losing one's way. Each man soon knew every wrinkle in the faces of the others. Within weeks conversation flagged as new topics for discussion became harder to find.[16]

Relations between the scientists and their commander were not even-tempered. Before winter set in, Borchgrevink's staff had formed an extremely negative opinion of their leader, the roots of which went back to the incident at Madeira. The researchers were infuriated at what they perceived was Borchgrevink's overreaction to their tardy return to the steamer. In the heat of that moment Evans had become angry and Borchgrevink had countered by threatening to fire him. Colbeck had incurred Borchgrevink's disfavor by coming to Evans's defense.[17]

The incident of the mail embargo exacerbated relations between the chief and his men. When Borchgrevink repeated his injunction against sending correspondence home, animosity became a fixed feature of the expedition.[18]

Borchgrevink's tendency to overreact when he perceived a problem and to turn against people when he felt injured made matters worse. As the ship passed through the ice pack, criticism of the route again by Colbeck put him out of favor briefly. At another point Borchgrevink turned his anger toward Jensen and contemplated replacing him as ship's captain with Colbeck, who, at the moment, was back in Borchgrevink's good graces. These vacillations undermined the men's confidence in their commander.

Once on the ice the scientists found other reasons to criticize their leader. Borchgrevink claimed to be a naturalist, yet his staff noted his inability to use scientific instruments. His haphazard approach to data collection angered the trained researchers. He could not be trusted to perform observations or to be careful in record keeping. At various times he broke instruments through misuse, confused meteorological records, and even allowed the chronometers to run down. His undisciplined behavior regarding meteorological records so exasperated Bernacchi that at one point he told Borchgrevink that he wanted no further part in the weather record keeping. Indeed, Bernacchi hoped Borchgrevink would make no mention of him in connection with the expedition.[19]

Borchgrevink was aware of his staff's opinion of him, and his reaction only exacerbated the problem. Increasingly, he felt that his assistants were turning against him and attempting to undermine his authority. In mid-June he produced a paper, written in Norwegian, that he claimed had been prepared by Newnes and his attorney. The note stated that to criticize the commander or to induce others to do so was mutiny. He showed the document first to several Norwegians who were playing cards at the table. When he presented it to the English members of the staff, he announced that mutiny would carry a punishment of fifteen years' imprisonment once the expedition returned to England. Bernacchi could barely control his anger. In his journal he claimed that the note was a forgery and that the contract was too vague and its legality too questionable to have been drawn up by Newnes and his lawyer. Bernacchi saw the paper as an attempt by Borchgrevink to frighten the staff and took it as "an insult I shall never forgive."[20]

Borchgrevink was not finished. The same evening, he dismissed Colbeck from the expedition. Henceforth Colbeck was to be merely a guest of Borchgrevink and was forbidden from engaging in work. If Colbeck admitted past mistakes and apologized, however, Borchgrevink was willing to reinstate him. Colbeck replied that he was not aware of any transgressions and that he had always endeavored to do what was asked of him. Borchgrevink's response has not survived but was characterized by Bernacchi as "vulgar and insolent."[21]

Bernacchi questioned Borchgrevink about the purported mutiny, particularly the legality of Borchgrevink's document:

I think that I may safely say that I have never before been so deeply affronted, nor do I think has any civilian member of any former scientific staff been so treated. As you know, I first offered my services as a volunteer but was compelled to accept a remuneration, that being a condition, so that I had no mercenary end in view nor did I seek the acquisition of cheap notoriety. I joined out of a genuine regard for the scientific work to be done on such an expedition and out of a desire to see for myself the polar regions of the Antarctic, and I think in all honesty you must admit that I have entered with enthusiasm into the above mentioned work, have always shown you due deference and courtesy and obeyed your commands according to my letter of agreement with you, so that why I should be subjected to insults I utterly fail to comprehend.[22]

Borchgrevink apologized to Bernacchi, stating that the document was not meant to apply to him. Borchgrevink revealed that he was aware of the animosity toward him. Bernacchi suggested that the ill will was merely temporary and would pass if Borchgrevink were not so antagonistic to his staff, and the Tasmanian urged the commander to make a reconciliation with Colbeck.[23]

The stalemate between Colbeck and Borchgrevink continued for another week, finally ending when the latter handed Colbeck a prayer book. Inside the volume was a short note offering a reconciliation, which Colbeck accepted. After a conversation outside the hut that evening sealed the rapprochement, Borchgrevink announced it to the group. Yet he gained no stature in the eyes of Bernacchi, who thought Borchgrevink had overplayed the entire incident. Indeed, Bernacchi's disregard for his chief is indicated by the reference in his journal to Borchgrevink as "L'enfant."[24] This continued ill will between staff and leader formed the backdrop for the winter's activities.

Borchgrevink led a series of sledging parties throughout the dark months to explore the region around Cape Adare. On 21 July he launched a sojourn to Possession Island, taking with him Fougner, the two Lapps, and thirty dogs. It was an arduous task in an Antarctic winter. Pressure ridges made the going slow and difficult. Temperatures during this journey hovered around −15 degrees Fahrenheit. The men slept directly on the frozen sea at night, occasionally doing without the tent and sleeping curled up in the snow or on top of the sledges to facilitate a quick escape in the event of danger. The pack ice wore out the rudders of the sledges. That, combined with the appearance of open water between them and Possession Island, ended the adventure. The party turned north toward Camp Ridley. One evening while returning to their headquarters, the two Lapps went hunting. Their uncanny ability to locate game was demonstrated again, although this time they used a different method. Fougner and Borchgrevink were stunned to see them approaching the tent herding before them a seal, like a cow being driven to market. Slaughtered, the animal provided a feast for the entire party, including the dogs. The next day the men proceeded through a strong wind and bitter cold to the safety of the hut.[25]

Between this sojourn and the next sledging trip, an incident occurred that nearly spelled disaster for the shore party. On 24 July the crew was awakened by smoke in the hut. A fire had started after Colbeck left a candle burning when he went out to take meteorological readings. The flame ignited the pine wall, but a quick response prevented the destruction of the lodging. To lose the hut would have been a catastrophe, as no materials existed at Cape Adare to replace it. To prevent a recurrence, extra precautions were taken and a cache of emergency supplies was stored on the cape to enable the men to survive the loss of the buildings.[26]

On 26 July, anticipating the return of the sun the following day, Borchgrevink led a foray into Robertson Bay. This was the beginning of an extensive exploration of its western reaches, a project that occupied a good deal of Borchgrevink's attention for the ensuing two months. The commander chose Evans and the two Lapps as companions, an honor Evans gladly would have declined. Crossing the ice, Borchgrevink decided that they lacked certain provisions and sent Evans back to obtain them while he and the Lapps continued toward their goal. Because the ice was riddled with pressure ridges, progress was slow. From the 28th to the 30th the three were confined to their tent by a terrible storm, but on the 31st they came to an island that Borchgrevink named for the duke of York. For the next week the group explored the area near the island and constructed a temporary shelter out of sledges and sealskins. Concerned that the additional supplies had not arrived, the party turned back to Camp Ridley on 4 August, a journey made in temperatures ranging down to −52 degrees Fahrenheit.[27]

On returning to base, Borchgrevink discovered that in his absence storms had prevented his staff from reaching him with supplies. After a brief stay at Camp Ridley, he returned to Duke of York Island, where his men constructed a stone hut in a sheltered area. Although primitively built, the structure was soon buried by snow, which provided insulation and made it habitable. By keeping a blubber fire going, the travelers raised the inside temperature to the freezing point. Borchgrevink had stores brought to the area, which he named Mid-Winter Camp; he spent much of August and September there. Ostensively, he was at Duke of York Island to explore, but both the scientists and their commander appreciated the separation that helped temper the mood of antagonism. Most often Borchgrevink was there in the company of the two Lapps. While living at Mid-Winter Camp, he explored Geikie Land, Crescent Bay, Colbeck Bay, and the Dugdale and Murray glaciers. Near the Dugdale Glacier on 11 September he killed a female seal in which he found a nearly full-term pup. The young animal rolled onto the ice, apparently healthy. Eventually, it was taken to Camp Ridley.[28]

During one of his visits to Mid-Winter Camp, Savio nearly lost his life. The Lapp had gone into a crevassed area without the precaution of roping up. Suddenly, the snow gave way beneath him, and after plunging sixty feet, he landed head-first, wedged into a crevasse. Three feet to the right no barrier existed; had he plummeted in that direction he would have fallen into what appeared to be a bottomless pit. Only his ability to keep his wits saved his life. Slowly, he maneuvered until he was upright. The ice offered no purchase for him to climb, but he used a small knife to carve a tiny toehold, and by bracing his back against one wall of the crevasse and cutting steps for footholds, he was able to climb to the surface. There Borchgrevink discovered him in a state of utter exhaustion.[29]

Part of Borchgrevink's motivation for exploring Duke of York Island was the hope that precious metals would be found. In fact, he discovered what he believed to be gold, a claim his scientists quickly and correctly dismissed as false. Undaunted, he spoke at Camp Ridley of the importance of the gold find to Antarctic exploration and how he planned on working with Newnes to exploit this opportunity. To his staff this was another example of Borchgrevink the dreamer, a man unqualified to lead a scientific endeavor. To safeguard his discovery, Borchgrevink "took possession" of Duke of York Island for Sir George Newnes under the protection of the

British flag. This action was greeted by Bernacchi and Colbeck with stifled snickers.[30]

Bernacchi believed that these excursions to Duke of York Island detracted from the real work of the expedition; Borchgrevink was wasting time and expending valuable supplies on a foolish project. The Tasmanian resented having to interrupt his magnetic and meteorological observations to make runs to Mid-Winter Camp to assist in Borchgrevink's folly. Moreover, Bernacchi believed that Borchgrevink spent time on the island to escape the others and to drink. The Tasmanian felt certain that the leader's inebriation was the cause of the deplorable condition of the sledges and instruments he found when he visited Mid-Winter Camp.[31]

Throughout the winter and into the early spring a routine was established at Camp Ridley. The chores—gathering ice to be melted for water, mending and repairing equipment—went on daily. The hut itself was serviceable. As storms packed the snow around it, the building became better insulated, although the drifts eventually necessitated tunneling a path to the outside.

Except for Hanson, the group was blessed with good health. Klovstad carefully monitored the condition of the crew, noting the weight, strength, and size of each man. The doctor's records indicated that the heart rates of the staff tended to slow during the dark winter months. Though some understandable homesickness occurred, the wholesale depression that plagued the *Belgica* was not evident. In general, the Lapps suffered less from the ill effects of the long winter night; that seemed natural, given their experience with Arctic conditions in their homeland. Because the group accepted the idea that scurvy was caused by poorly preserved foods, the doctor examined each tin before it was served. The incorporation of fresh meat and fish on a regular basis contributed to the health of the men by providing vitamins that the canning process had destroyed. In view of the medical difficulties of other expeditions of the time, the hardiness of the *Southern Cross* staff must be credited, in part, to its diet.[32]

Meals were surprisingly brief affairs. Over time, after-dinner conversation dwindled. The menu was quite varied, although the explorers tired of tinned food, as had the crew of the *Belgica*. At first Ellifen, the cook, had difficulty pleasing the staff, but the absence of complaints about food indicates his eventual success. Although he never mastered the art of

English pudding—once on board during a heavy sea with the ship listing considerably, one of the Englishmen chided the cook by suggesting that Ellifen pass the pudding windward—he became adept at cooking seal and penguin. Making penguin palatable was an accomplishment.[33]

Aside from the scientific work, the men passed their days at the hut in a variety of activities. When weather permitted, skiing provided recreation for the English and especially the Norwegians. Storytelling was a popular pastime, with a tendency to the fanciful. Here Evans demonstrated considerable prowess, relating tales of his adventures in Canada and his Iles Kerguelen whaling experiences. Any excuse was made for a break in the routine, and birthday celebrations became a standard diversion. Toasts and flag flying were used to salute the birthdays of Newnes, Queen Victoria, the duke of York, and the Princess of Wales and to celebrate Norwegian holidays.[34]

Occasionally, various members of the shore party entertained by lecturing, singing, or reading aloud. Borchgrevink enjoyed lecturing, although his staff found the talks tiresome. Singing was popular, and Savio and Must could be counted on to add a Lapp song. Grog and "a pleasant smoke" followed the entertainment. Reading was a favorite activity, and the library contained many volumes on exploration. An indication of Borchgrevink's excellent preparations is that his men were not obsessed with food, as the crews on other expeditions had been when horrid food or starvation rations caused them to think of little else. On less well equipped expeditions, a cookbook was often the most popular reading material. Chess had a limited following; it was not one of Borchgrevink's strengths. Card games, especially whist, occupied many hours. Often the losers performed the kitchen duties. One of the most popular escapes was sleep—naps helped to while away the long hours.[35]

Life in the hut had its drawbacks. Limited opportunities existed for washing either clothing or the body. Most of the men celebrated New Year's by turning their shirts inside out, exposing a different side to their skin. The Lapps were the most enterprising. Savio built an igloo and fashioned a makeshift sauna that he used during the winter. The need to eliminate drafts resulted in a fairly stuffy atmosphere inside the hut, a condition not improved by the regular pipe smoking. Finally, as spring arrived, bringing warmer weather, the men discovered that the structures were built over guano beds, the smell of which permeated their rooms on warmer days.[36]

Caring for the samoyeds required considerable time. Any doubts about the value of these animals for transportation in South Polar regions were eliminated by the experiences of the *Southern Cross* expedition. The dogs performed well in all weather and terrain and proved that they were efficient beasts of burden. Since they ate food that was available locally, it was often possible when working near the coast to provide them with additional nourishment by killing penguins and seals. Requiring no manmade shelter, the samoyeds withstood the cold, preferring to bury themselves in the snow for warmth. Even a gale of several days caused no difficulty; the animals kept a hole open to breathe through as the snow formed a blanket over them. On occasion they were found after a storm frozen in the ice, but they were easily extricated with no ill effects.[37]

The samoyeds' tenacity and hardiness were incredible. The best example of their ability to adapt occurred in June when a dog returned to camp after it had been missing for two months and had been given up for lost. It came back healthy and without a weight loss, having apparently lived off seals and penguins.[38]

The ferocity needed to survive in the Antarctic winter occasionally displayed itself in relations among the animals. From time to time the pack would set on and kill one of its members. The victim was marked out beforehand and isolated from its peers. Sensing its future, the ostracized one would flee the camp area. As soon as it reappeared, the rest of the dogs would take out after it and devour it. Nothing the humans could do protected an animal from this fate.[39]

Despite these semiwild tendencies, man and dog often became friends. Although the samoyeds were originally the responsibility of the Lapps, the rest of the men became fond of individual dogs. Forming an attachment to the animals helped them fight the depression that isolation brought. When Fougner's favorite dog died, for example, he tried to hide his emotions, but the others noticed the care he took in carving a grave out of the frozen surface of Cape Adare. Questioned, Fougner explained his actions as necessary to prevent the other dogs from falling ill as a result of eating the carcass.[40]

The dogs more than repaid the several thousand pounds invested in them. Moreover, they bred in the Antarctic winter, thus providing the expedition with additional transport for the spring sledging season. That the debate over the use of dogs continued throughout the Heroic Era is an indication of the refusal of later explorers to profit from the lessons of the

Southern Cross. This first experiment with dogs on the Antarctic continent was an unqualified success.[41]

The crew could always rely on the mystery and beauty of the Antarctic to entertain them. Moonlight in winter was sufficient for walks along the cape. Curiously, in their evening peregrinations, the staff tended to stroll north. There was a never-ending array of natural wonders to observe, including the ice rafting in the bay, a phenomenon that overwhelmed the men with its power. The sight of the aurora or icebergs driven by currents into the teeth of a storm provided many hours of entertainment. The fascination that the Antarctic night sky held for the company was conveyed by Bernacchi:

> There is something particularly mystical and uncanny in the effect of the gray atmosphere of an Antarctic night through whose uncertain medium the cold white landscape looms as impalpable as the frontiers of a demon world. It was strange to watch the moon describing a complete circle in the sky, not setting for days at a time, but just coasting along the summits of the mountain ranges.[42]

Throughout the long night, thoughts of home were never completely absent. Bernacchi recorded one such memory in his journal: "The other day in turning over some old letters I came across a dried flower! A sweet scented carnation. Retained nearly all its subtle fragrance. I remember it was given to me on the day we left Melbourne. It was like a voice from another world."[43]

Despite this fascination with their surroundings, the men were simultaneously aware of the dangers of life in the Antarctic. The fire of 24 July was a spectacular example, but more common was the experience of Evans, who went out briefly during a storm to check the meteorological instruments and got lost when he let go of the guide rope between the hut and the weather station. After a three-hour search Fougner found him, exhausted and vomiting from the severe cold.[44]

Hanson's health had been a cause for concern through the winter. In early July he temporarily took a turn for the worse, and in September, when he began to decline again, it became clear that he would not live long. Because the doctor was not certain of the nature of the illness, little could be done. In his last weeks Hanson vomited regularly, especially at mealtimes. Bernacchi offered his less drafty bunk to Hanson, but even with constant care the invalid did not improve. As the end drew near, the rest of the party slept in tents, leaving the hut to Klovstad and Hanson. Early in the morning of 14 October the men were awakened and informed that Hanson's death was imminent. Hanson was particularly anxious about his zoological research, urging that the work be continued and the specimens analyzed after the ship's return to England. He gave his private papers to Klovstad, turned over his scientific notes to Borchgrevink, and thanked each man and bade them farewell. He kept his spirits up to the end. Shortly before he died, he turned to Fougner and said facetiously, "What would you say now, small boys, if I suddenly got up and walked outside?" Fougner replied, "I cannot believe, Hanson, that you are so near to death." Hanson rejoined, "Oh yes, I am sure of it. I know the doctor, he is a man of his word."[45]

Half an hour before Hanson died, Evans captured and brought him the first penguin of the season, the return of which Hanson had eagerly awaited. "Is he full grown?" Hanson asked. Then, just before the end, he said to Fougner, "It is not so hard to die in a strange land, it is just like saying good-bye to one's friends when starting on a long journey."[46]

As he had requested, Hanson was buried at the summit of Cape Adare. Digging a grave proved nearly impossible in the frozen earth, and eventually the men resorted to explosives to create a shallow chamber. Borchgrevink read a funeral service, and the Lapps recited their own ritual words over the body.[47]

With the coming of spring the staff engaged in further research on fauna and undertook more sledging trips. Borchgrevink resumed his journeys to Duke of York Island, where Evans and Colbeck studied the penguin rookery in October. This visit added to Evans's extensive notes on penguins; unfortunately, these data were lost at the conclusion of the expedition. The following month, traveling across heavily rafted ice, Borchgrevink moved east from Cape Adare to explore the sea. Because the ice was beginning to break up, he and Must slept in their kayaks. Within two days they were forced to turn back, as the ice was becoming too thin and the sea appeared to be opening to the east.[48]

The last incursion into Robertson Bay to study birds and secure eggs was made in early December 1899. On this sojourn Klovstad found three different varieties of insects living in moss in Geikie Land. This first discovery of insects within the Antarctic Circle ranked as one of the scientific triumphs of the expedition.[49]

In the vicinity of Cape Adare the staff found increased opportunity for research with the reappearance of the local fauna. Penguins by the millions arrived for the brief summer. For fourteen days they formed a solid line as they marched to the rookery from the sea. As soon as eggs appeared, the men began collecting them, both for specimens and for the larder. Given the uncertainty of the ship's return, they prudently gathered more than four thousand eggs as a food stockpile. Roast penguin, which began to appear more often on the dinner menu, was a welcome change after the winter.[50]

In December the crew hoped to witness a solar eclipse, which was expected on the 3d. No eclipse had been observed that far south, and it would have provided the scientists with an exact longitude for Cape Adare. Unfortunately, the sun was obscured during the entire eclipse.[51]

Whereas August was the coldest month, January was the most depressing. The reappearance of the *Southern Cross* was eagerly expected; its failure to arrive brought a daily disappointment that grew into a fear that the men might be marooned for at least a second winter, a prospect all dreaded. The dismay began to become noticeable at the end of November when the sea around Cape Adare remained solid ice. The break-up of the pack in December brought no appearance of the ship, although Borchgrevink did not anticipate its arrival until New Year's. He wagered five pounds that the vessel would return before 1 January 1900. Gradually, a sense of gloom settled over the party; the feeling of being imprisoned affected the men, and production declined. They found it more difficult to motivate themselves, and journal writing became less regular.[52]

Knowing that Ross had sighted Cape Adare on 11 January 1841 and seeing the open sea offshore in January 1900 increased fear that the *Southern Cross* had been lost. A mid-January storm, the fiercest of the year, kept the residents hutbound, a setback that did not improve morale, which Bernacchi described as "less than zero." Each day the pilgrimage to the observation point ended with the announcement that no vessel was in sight.[53]

Early on the morning of 28 January, when Colbein Ellifen left the hut to get a bag of coal, he looked up to see a creature approaching him; dazed, he finally recognized Captain Jensen. The captain threw open the door and awakened the rest of the party by tossing a mailbag on the table and announcing, "Post!" After greetings all around, the men retired to read their letters. News of the outside world amazed them—for the first time they heard of the South African War and other events of the previous year.[54]

Borchgrevink decided to leave Camp Ridley as quickly as possible to explore the coast in the *Southern Cross*. Equipment and dogs were rapidly loaded. The last act before leaving the cape was to visit Hanson's grave, where they erected a large cross with a bronze plaque as a memorial.

Sailing south toward McMurdo Bay, Bernacchi reflected on the departure from Cape Adare in his journal: "We are not sorry to leave this gelid desolate spot, our place of abode for so many dreary months! May I never pass another twelve months, in similar surroundings and conditions."[55]

For two weeks the *Southern Cross* cruised from Cape Adare to the Bay of Whales. Possession Island, the object of an unsuccessful winter sledging journey, came into view on 3 February. A landing was made early on the 3d, but threatening weather prevented the recording of magnetic observations. Ashore the party proceeded to the tobacco tin, where Captain Kristensen of the *Antarctic* had left a message. Both box and note were found in perfect condition. The paper was read aloud and returned to its place with a second penciled statement signed by the group. Immediately, it was obvious that this would have been a better site for their winter headquarters than Cape Adare. The island was less exposed to the terrible winds that buffeted Camp Ridley and was less affected by local magnetic interferences.[56]

After a few hours at Possession Island the party sailed to Coulman Island, a forbidding landscape with cliffs rising perpendicularly out of the water. Undaunted, Borchgrevink, Bernacchi, and Colbeck made the first landing on the island in a small boat. This visit was even briefer than the previous stop. The hazards of reaching solid ground made it too risky to attempt to land the magnetic instruments. The shore party walked around for a few minutes, took several photographs, and returned to the ship. As the *Southern Cross* passed the tip of the island, Borchgrevink named the spit Cape Constance for his wife.[57]

The steamer continued south, stopping along the edge of the ice to examine a rookery and make magnetic observations. Borchgrevink angered Bernacchi by asking the latter to leave his magnetic work, which Bernacchi considered important, to photograph a seal. Colbeck completed the dip observation and Bernacchi renewed the declination measurement before the two men returned to the ship.[58]

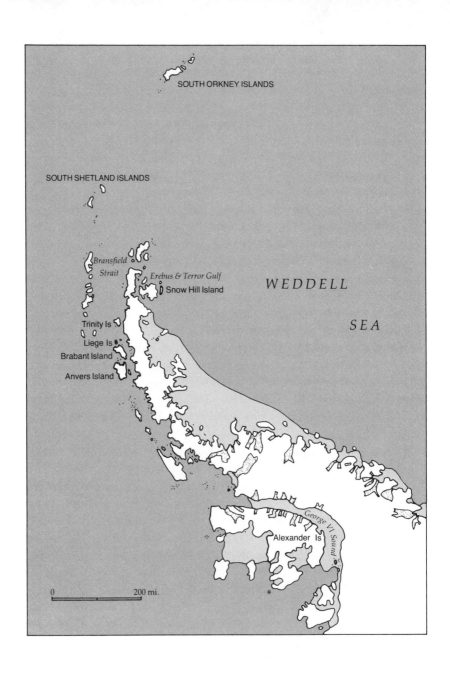

SOUTH ORKNEY ISLANDS

SOUTH SHETLAND ISLANDS

*Bransfield
Strait*

Erebus & Terror Gulf

Snow Hill Island

WEDDELL

SEA

Trinity Is

Liege Is

Brabant Island

Anvers Island

George VI Sound

Alexander Is

0   200 mi.

Map 4
Antarctic Peninsula

The *Southern Cross* steamed into Wood Bay on 5 February. Even more than Possession Island, this sheltered harbor appeared to be an excellent place for a base camp; it was the only site in South Victoria Land that could protect a vessel from ice damage over the winter. Moreover, it would have been a better starting point for a trek to the South Magnetic Pole. While the others went exploring, Colbeck and Bernacchi continued their magnetic work.[59]

The party arrived at Franklin Island on 9 February. Again the scientists took readings, although a heavy snow prevented a sighting of the sun for declination calculations. Borchgrevink decided to return to this location on the way home to complete the observations. While on the island Fougner made some interesting discoveries of shallow-water fauna which added to the studies undertaken at Cape Adare.[60]

From Franklin Island the ship steamed to Cape Crozier, bypassing McMurdo Bay. En route Borchgrevink named a cape on Franklin Island for Bernacchi. Landing at Cape Tennyson, Borchgrevink took with him Jensen, Colbeck, and two Norwegian sailors. Little was accomplished, and Jensen and Borchgrevink had a narrow escape when a calving iceberg sent out an eight-foot wave that overtook the two men onshore and nearly washed them out to sea. At the time of the landing it appeared that Cape Tennyson might be the furthest south this expedition would reach. Bernacchi angrily noted in his journal that, on this English journey, four of the five men furthest south were Norwegians. To Bernacchi it was an intentional slight by Borchgrevink.[61]

Passing Cape Crozier, the men had their first view of the Great Ice Barrier. This crew was as awed as Ross's men had been by the sight; the perpendicular wall of ice 150 feet high overwhelmed them. The *Southern Cross* sailed along the barrier for eight days while fog hampered its progress. The mist reduced visibility nearly to zero, although up in the crow's nest it was often clear. The presence of icebergs also required a cautious tracking along the shore, and several times only a quick reaction at the helm avoided a collision.[62]

Borchgrevink believed the Great Ice Barrier to be the edge of a large ice sheet running to the sea from the land near the South Pole. Bernacchi essentially agreed, rejecting the theory that the barrier was the edge of a polar ice cap. But Bernacchi erred in thinking that the barrier ran for fifty miles inland, beyond which lay open sea before one reached the pole.

Bernacchi also believed that no Antarctic continent existed, only a series of islands.[63]

Proceeding cautiously eastward for several days, the crew had a limited view of the barrier through the fog. While enveloped in the mist, the *Southern Cross* established a new furthest south, eclipsing Ross's mark. A ceremony celebrated the achievement, with the men of the forecastle invited to the salon to toast their success. Borchgrevink marked the occasion with a typically long-winded speech. Then, on 16 February, the weather cleared to reveal an inlet, a break in the barrier.[64]

During the Heroic Era, Shackleton named this harbor, surrounded by ice, the Bay of Whales. Borchgrevink and Jensen debated the wisdom of taking the steamer into the opening but decided to risk having the harbor suddenly close with ice, trapping the ship. Inside the bay the barrier sloped to the water's edge, and a landing was accomplished without difficulty. The entire crew disembarked to have a photograph taken at the southernmost point achieved by any vessel.[65]

To establish a new furthest south Borchgrevink, Colbeck, and Savio made a run on 17 February with dogs and skis across the barrier. At that point the surface allowed easy travel. They continued about ten miles south and returned that afternoon. A second brief journey was made by Bernacchi, Fougner, second engineer Julius Johanesen, and Evans early on the 19th. They skied over the ice several miles to observe seals that were about an hour from the vessel, but their foray was cut short by a blast from the ship's whistle that signaled them to return. The *Southern Cross* steamed out of the Bay of Whales a little after one o'clock in the afternoon, proceeding with difficulty because of the slush that had formed in the inlet. Ramming its way through the new ice, the barque departed from the barrier and set a course for the north and home.[66]

The *Southern Cross* steamed directly to Franklin Island, where it was hoped that several days of magnetic observations could be made, but bad weather prevented a landing. Because of the lateness of the season, Borchgrevink abandoned further exploration and sailed for Tasmania.[67]

The four-week voyage back to civilization was frightful. After passing the Antarctic Circle on 3 March 1900, the *Southern Cross* encountered terrible storms that at times drove it back toward the Antarctic. Finally, it arrived at Port Ross, Auckland Island, on 21 March, where the crew secured fresh meat and cleared the boilers in preparation for the voyage to Stewart Island. There Borchgrevink cabled Newnes: "Object of

108

the expedition carried out. South Magnetic Pole located. Farthest south with sledge record 78° 50'. Zoologist Hanson dead. All well on board."[68] Borchgrevink proceeded by schooner to Hobart, where he was reunited with the *Southern Cross* ten days later. A thanksgiving service at Hobart cathedral welcomed the explorers.[69]

Borchgrevink and the scientists departed for England by passenger ship, and the *Southern Cross* followed at summer's end. Borchgrevink's reception in England was subdued; preparations for the *Discovery* expedition took precedence over the explorers' return. When Bernacchi and Borchgrevink published their accounts of the *Southern Cross*, Bernacchi's was widely praised but Borchgrevink's was criticized for its errors and journalistic style.[70]

The scientific results of the journey were published by the British Museum in 1902, by which time the *Discovery* had sailed and usurped much of the attention paid to Antarctic affairs. The most easily overlooked achievement of the *Southern Cross* expedition was its proof that humans could endure an Antarctic winter, although the choice of Cape Adare as a camp made that experience more harrowing than it might have been. Cape Adare is located in an area of perennially low barometric pressure and is in line with the path of storms blowing off the continent from the southeast. These conditions were harsher than most on the Antarctic coast.

The meteorological records of the expedition covered the period from 18 February 1899 to 28 January 1900, giving weather observers nearly a full year of data. Readings had been taken by Bernacchi, Colbeck, Evans, Fougner, and Hanson every two hours.[71] The meteorological work of the *Southern Cross* staff confirmed John Murray's theory of a permanent anticyclonic area over Antarctica. The observations at Camp Ridley helped disprove the theory, put forth by Maury, that the Antarctic is an area of high humidity at the pole.[72]

The magnetic notes of Colbeck and Bernacchi were analyzed and published by Dr. Charles Chree for the Royal Society. Bernacchi and Colbeck had succeeded in their primary objective of locating the South Magnetic Pole. They were able to pinpoint it partially as a result of the observations taken en route from Cape Adare to the Great Ice Barrier in February 1900, but their inability to reach the pole detracted from their research. Throughout their stay at Cape Adare, the explorers had been cut off from the pole by impassable mountains.

The magnetic studies also provided insight into the aurora. Although Colbeck and Bernacchi knew that a direct relationship existed between terrestrial magnetism and this phenomenon, they were unable to determine the nature of the association. Similarly, they surmised a connection between terrestrial magnetism and sunspots, and although their research did not support any conclusions, it pointed the way for subsequent investigation.[73]

Before the voyage of the *Southern Cross* a controversy had raged over the existence of shallow-water fauna in southern latitudes. The scientists discovered many species of such animals; these findings opened the way for further study. The primitive state of Antarctic science is indicated by the way shallow-water fauna studies advanced in Borchgrevink's day. One of the first discoveries of these fauna occurred after a storm when the men, walking along the cape, found creatures that had been blown out of the water and had been immediately frozen to the ice onshore. Before this expedition many scientists had argued against the existence of shoreline ecosystems.[74]

Additional information regarding the bipolarity theory, according to which similar flora and fauna exist at the two poles, was discovered. The difference in fauna disproved the premise, but the staff gathered data that supported the assumptions regarding flora.[75]

Because of Hanson's fine reputation as an enthusiastic and careful observer, it was expected that much of the important work of the voyage would be in zoology. That the results in this area were disappointing created one of the greatest controversies of the expedition and the one that, more than any other, sullied Borchgrevink's reputation.

Until ill health stayed his efforts, Hanson had been an indefatigable worker, gathering and preserving examples for study in England and analyzing the species he encountered. Near the end of his life he had given Borchgrevink his scientific notebooks. Yet when the commander delivered the zoological collection to Robert Bowdler-Sharpe in the Natural History Section of the British Museum, only the sketchiest notes were included.

As the zoological collection was studied and the results prepared for publication, Bowdler-Sharpe was handicapped by the absence of documentation. Moreover, many specimens had deteriorated because of poor handling en route. In the *Report on the Collections of Natural History Made in the Antarctic Regions during the Voyage of the "Southern Cross,"* edited by E. Ray Lankester, director of the British Museum's Natural History

Museum at South Kensington, blame for the disappointing zoological results was placed on Borchgrevink.

Lankester insinuated that Borchgrevink lost Hanson's notes either intentionally or through carelessness. Not only the editor but the researchers who analyzed the specimens criticized the lack of commentary and the specimens' deteriorating condition. Bowdler-Sharpe attempted to overcome the scarcity of data by interviewing Evans and Bernacchi and by corresponding with Hanson's father and Professor Collett of Christiania University. The latter two men were able to assist because of information they had received in letters from Hanson. The fact that Evans's extensive account of penguins was lost while in the care of Borchgrevink lent credence to the allegations of carelessness.[76]

Lankester's criticism prompted an immediate but ill-advised and ill-conceived reply from Borchgrevink. In an exchange of letters to the editor of *The Times* each side attacked the other. In his opening salvo Borchgrevink claimed to have assisted Hanson, whom he referred to as his "taxidermist." Borchgrevink defended himself from what he considered Lankester's spiteful charges. He failed to address the lost notes and, by refusing to give sufficient credit to Hanson, succeeded only in portraying himself in the worst possible light.[77]

In a second letter Borchgrevink took credit for giving the *Southern Cross* collection to the British Museum even though the museum had nothing to do with the expedition. He denied having lost or misplaced Hanson's records, claiming that all documents were handed over to Bowdler-Sharpe except for some unimportant papers that Hanson had written in pencil on "sanitary paper." He refuted Bernacchi's claim to have seen such notebooks transferred to his care by insisting that no one except Klovstad and Fougner had been present at the time. Borchgrevink lowered the standard of the debate by taking all accusations as direct insults and by engaging in personal attacks on his opponents.[78]

Lankester replied in kind. Defending Hanson as a fine scientist, he reminded readers that Hanson had been the only qualified zoologist on the expedition as well as an "industrious observer" who kept detailed records. He ridiculed the idea that writing notes on thin paper somehow diminished their importance and castigated Borchgrevink as "a person with whom one would gladly have no dealings."[79]

In a second letter Lankester asserted that Borchgrevink had criticized the British Museum's study of the *Southern Cross* collections without citing specific objections. He quoted a statement by Bowdler-Sharpe that none of Hanson's documents had been given to him by Borchgrevink. Bowdler-Sharpe recounted his interview with Borchgrevink in October 1901 in which the latter had been urged to turn over all materials. Again Borchgrevink denied the existence of such records and criticized Bowdler-Sharpe for taking the word of the expedition's staff over his own. From his interviews with Bernacchi, Colbeck, and Evans, Bowdler-Sharpe was convinced that six or seven zoological notebooks had existed and that they had been given to Borchgrevink by Hanson on his deathbed; Borchgrevink denied it. For Borchgrevink "now [to] dismiss Hanson's work as that of a taxidermist after failing to produce his papers is not," Lankester retorted, "under the circumstances, surprising, though not commendable."[80]

Borchgrevink attempted to obscure the question of Hanson's missing records by claiming that the true issue was an intentional, personal attack on himself. By choosing obfuscation, Borchgrevink failed to convince anyone of his innocence. He quoted letters from Bowdler-Sharpe thanking him for the collection, complimenting the quality of the specimens, and praising him for the expedition's excellent research. Borchgrevink felt slighted despite his devotion to the British Museum: "I am practically the generous donor who has received nothing but ingratitude and insults from those who benefited by my gifts—the result of my life's work."[81] His reputation was never cleared of the shadow cast over it by the debate over the lost notebooks.

Borchgrevink's leadership was also subjected to extensive criticism following his return, and his achievements were largely ignored at the time. Clearly, he was not as able a scientist as Colbeck or Bernacchi. He had a natural curiosity but lacked the discipline and training that shaped a careful and prudent observer. In his relations with his staff Borchgrevink's inexperience as a commander was a disadvantage; nothing in his past indicated he could command men under difficult circumstances. His life before 1898 indicates that he was a handsome figure who exploited a minimum of Antarctic experience to maximum advantage. The skills he used in his relentless pursuit of the capital for his venture did not help him direct the enterprise.

Borchgrevink's braggadocio did not endear the commander to his staff. Bravado and competence might well be valued characteristics in an Antarctic expedition leader. Borchgrevink's problem was that he was perceived to have the bravado but not the competence. Polar exploration at the turn of the century was not a place for timid leaders. Then as now a healthy self-confidence has its place in an expedition. Borchgrevink's failing was that, unlike Sir Ernest Shackleton, he could not back up his conceit with action. Men followed Shackleton with devotion not only because he acted like a commander but because the force of his personality made him one. Borchgrevink never succeeded in establishing his moral right to lead. Because Shackleton was a successful expedition director without being a scientist, lack of scientific training cannot excuse Borchgrevink's failure.

Without question, however, Borchgrevink was the victim of national and linguistic prejudice. Once Bernacchi and the others became aware of Borchgrevink's scientific pretensions and questioned his capacity to command, it became easier to attack the leader on other grounds. Bernacchi's diary contains numerous references to Borchgrevink's faulty English and focused on several instances of national differences.[82]

Although Hanson was Norwegian, he was well liked by the English staff. A scientist respected for the quality of his work, he also spoke fluent English. He was hard-working, another quality greatly admired, whereas Borchgrevink was seen as habitually lazy.

In the final event, Borchgrevink must be given credit for launching a private enterprise, staffing it with excellent personnel, and except for Hanson's unavoidable death, bringing the entire crew back safely. His staff accomplished a good deal, given the difficult conditions at Camp Ridley. Borchgrevink's most serious mistake was the selection of Cape Adare when other locations would have provided his men with a better locale in which to work. Unlike the *Discovery*, which was the last of the old-style, overmanned, overly costly expeditions characteristic of nineteenth-century British polar exploration, the *Southern Cross* presaged the Antarctic forays of the twentieth century—small, efficient, and led by a single man fired by a vision to explore the unknown.

EIGHT

Lessons Not Learned

Because the men in British geographic circles refused to profit from the knowledge gained during the ten years before the *Discovery* sailed, they squandered the lessons of the 1890s. Instead, the prime movers of the *Discovery* took the Arctic adventures of the 1850s as their model. Rather than building on the experiences of the immediate past, the planners repeated the mistakes of fifty years and condemned British Antarctic exploration to tragedy in the second decade of the twentieth century.

The progenitor of the *Discovery*, Sir Clements Markham, had used the Royal Geographical Society to achieve his dream of exploring the South Polar regions. In his quest to finance a naval venture, he had turned to other British scientific organizations, principally the Royal Society. In doing so, he successfully campaigned for Treasury support to supplement private funds. The intervention of the Royal Society had been crucial in persuading Balfour's cabinet to underwrite the adventure. The government recognized the Royal Society and the Royal Geographical Society as guardians of the finances for the endeavor. Once money was ensured, Markham and the RGS were left in a partnership with the Royal Society that nearly wrecked the enterprise before the first sail was rigged on the *Discovery*.

Markham, the inveterate bureaucrat, decided that a joint committee was ideal to direct the myriad of details that would transform his ideas into reality. While the two societies retained ultimate control, each delegated day-to-day authority to the committee, a move that handicapped the enterprise. In November 1900 the commander assumed responsibility, but by then the expedition was behind schedule in its preparations. Recent ventures had demonstrated that such undertakings needed a single leader with the power to make decisions. Of the expeditions of the period 1891–1922, the *Discovery* was the only one directed by committee. The tardy appointment of Robert Falcon Scott to supervise all day-to-day operations meant that the *Discovery* was constantly behind schedule in its preparations to depart.

From the outset two factions existed in the joint committee, and wrangling over the conduct of the project became the norm. One group stressed the geographical aspects of the expedition; the other felt empirical inquiry should be the focus of the endeavor.

The groups clashed over the role of the director of the civilian staff. The Royal Society contingent wanted the scientists to have unfettered control, with the naval commander in charge of the vessel but not of the shore party or the research. Edward Poulton, professor of zoology at Oxford and one of the leaders of the Royal Society's forces, even suggested that a civilian be named to head the entire endeavor, including command of the ship, but the naval hands on the committee convinced him that this was counter to British law. Markham envisioned a scientific team led by a civilian, as in the case of the *Challenger*, where Wyville Thomson had held this position. That voyage had been under the command of Sir George Nares, who sought the advice of Thomson on research matters. For a time the issue of the relative roles of commander and scientific director was avoided.[1]

Contemporaneous expeditions reinforced the lessons of the 1890s, showing that a civilian leader could achieve splendid results, as Professor Carl Chun had in managing the *Valdivia* in 1898. The captain of the *Valdivia*, Adalbert Krech, took his orders from Chun. Borchgrevink had directed the *Southern Cross*, supervising Bernhard Jensen, who was in charge of the ship itself. The Germans chose an eminent geologist, Erich von Drygalski (1865–1949), to oversee all aspects of the *Gauss*, and the Swedish expedition sailed under the command of noted scientist Otto Nordenskjöld.[2] Finally, the Scottish national expedition, launched a year after the *Discovery*, was also headed by a civilian, William S. Bruce, whose stature as a polar researcher made him a logical choice to command a

British expedition. Thus three of four voyages in the opening years of the twentieth century were under civilian command. In failing to follow this example, the joint committee ignored the valuable lessons of the 1890s.

The men chosen as commander and scientific head soon renewed the quarrel over the role each would play on the *Discovery*. Robert Falcon Scott (1868–1912), a lieutenant in the Royal Navy, was named commander. The joint committee chose J. W. Gregory (1864–1932), a scientist and explorer of considerable note, as director of the scientific staff. Educated at the University of London, he later worked at the British Museum's Geology Department. After participating in an expedition to British East Africa in 1892, he reorganized that group and directed it to the region of Mount Kenya, where important geographical and geological studies were carried out. In this adventure he demonstrated substantial ability to lead men in difficult circumstances. He followed this triumph with a campaign near Spitsbergen. His expertise in geology was deemed excellent preparation for Antarctic work. Shortly after his appointment to the *Discovery*, Gregory was named professor of geology at Melbourne. Without question he was eminently qualified to oversee the scientific program of the venture.[3]

Scott lacked a background in science and polar matters. A torpedo officer, he was Markham's choice, and the president of the RGS had to overcome the objections of a faction within the joint committee to persuade that body to ratify his nominee. Years before, Markham had detailed the qualifications he sought in a commander:

> He must be a naval officer, he must be in the regular line and not in the surveying branch, and he must be young. These are essentials. Such a commander should be a good sailor with some experience of ships under sail, a navigator with a knowledge of surveying, and he should be of a scientific turn of mind. He must have imagination and be capable of enthusiasm. His temperament must be cool, he must be calm yet quick and decisive in action, a man of resource, tactful and sympathetic.[4]

The selection of Scott was inconsistent with the RGS council's rejection two years earlier of Borchgrevink's request for assistance to launch his expedition. Borchgrevink had been turned down on the grounds that the commander of such a venture ought to be a scientist.[5]

In nominating Scott, Markham overlooked the one Briton best qualified to direct an Antarctic venture at the opening of the twentieth century: William S. Bruce. The lessons of the previous decade pointed to Bruce as an ideal leader for the *Discovery*. Described by a biographer as "the first of the scientist explorers," he was an obvious choice either to command or to supervise the scientific staff.[6] His activities on the *Balaena*, along with his work in Franz Josef Land on the Jackson-Harmsworth expedition, gave him a greater range of experience than any other candidate. Between voyages he had worked at the Ben Nevis Observatory, gathering data under extremely harsh climatic conditions. His interest in the Antarctic was well known; he had applied for a position on Bull's *Antarctic* but had been prevented from joining the voyage by his inability to rendezvous with the ship at Melbourne. This failure had given Borchgrevink his opportunity. Bruce had petitioned for money for a small foray to South Georgia Island and had gone to the Arctic when no good opportunity to go south presented itself. Borchgrevink recognized Bruce's ability and asked Mill to persuade the Scot to accompany the *Southern Cross*. That Bruce chose instead to go to the Arctic is more a reflection on Borchgrevink than an indication of a diminished interest in the Antarctic on Bruce's part.[7]

When Bruce heard of the forthcoming national Antarctic expedition, he offered Markham his services. In his letter Bruce demonstrated that he had spent the previous seven years preparing for such an opportunity. He referred to his considerable experience and his scholarly work, both of which would be valuable to Markham's venture. In a subsequent note Bruce added a list of his references, which included some of the most important contemporary figures in polar exploration: the Prince of Monaco, Sir John Murray (knighted in 1898), Dr. Alexander Buchan, J. Y. Buchanan, Fridtjof Nansen, Andrew Coats, and Alfred Harmsworth. Markham replied in April 1899 that he would be glad to meet with Bruce in London, adding that no decisions had been made about personnel for the venture.[8]

For eleven months Bruce's place on the staff remained undecided. Bruce feared that Markham was prejudiced against him because of his nationality. Certainly, Bruce had not always curried favor with the president of the RGS. When Bruce returned from the Arctic, he had presented the first results of the Jackson-Harmsworth adventure to the Royal Scottish Geographical Society instead of to the RGS, a slight Markham had noted. As H. R. Mill cautioned Bruce:

You are too unworldly, and have too high an idea of the unselfishness of the scientific societies. The RGS quite naturally wished to have the first news of your Arctic work and as you went in my place I had expected you would have given the paper to the society that would not let me go! However I know you did not mean to slight the RGS and I still take pleasure in seeing the Scottish Society getting a good thing. But you don't realize how necessary it is to keep on cordial terms with such powerful corporations as the RGS if you hope to enlist their aid in helping you to subsequent expeditions.[9]

Markham also may have had reservations about such a strong, superbly trained, well-connected person becoming a rival to Scott. Clearly, Bruce's veiled threat to launch his own expedition discouraged Markham from promoting his candidacy.[10]

The matter was resolved in the spring of 1900 with Bruce's announcement that he was leading his own endeavor, scheduled to depart for the Antarctic in 1902. Like Markham and others, Mill was surprised by Bruce's sudden declaration that his expedition had secured financial backing. Mill congratulated Bruce, but Markham took the news as yet another threat to his endeavor. He wrote Bruce:

I am sorry to hear that an attempt is to be made at Edinburgh to divert funds from the Antarctic expedition in order to get up a rival enterprise. Such a course will be most prejudicial to the expedition which is much in need of more funds. A second ship is not the least required. It is not true that the whole area is not provided for. If the Germans do not undertake the Weddell Quadrant, it will be undertaken by our expedition as a first object. I do not understand why this mischievous rivalry should have been started, but I trust that you will not connect yourself with it.[11]

Markham's refusal to consider Bruce denied the *Discovery* an experienced, competent leader. In view of what was accomplished by the Scottish National Antarctic Expedition operating on severely restricted funds, it is clear that the results of the *Discovery* would have been far greater had the endeavor been directed by a scientist of Bruce's stature.

Instead, Markham kept to his choice of Scott. Regardless of other possible reasons, Scott met Markham's overarching criterion as a commander: he was a naval officer. It was a further advantage that he was young and willing to take direction from the old Arctic hands who populated British exploring circles.[12]

A struggle in the joint committee over the instructions to be given to the commander and the scientific director erupted in February 1901, less than six months before the expedition was to sail. The joint committee revised the guidelines for the two principals of the *Discovery*. Poulton's faction apparently had triumphed, and Gregory was to receive virtual control of the venture, as manifested by the geologist's command of the land station to be established in the Antarctic. Under these terms Scott and the naval personnel would have been reduced to ferrying the scientists to and from the ice, giving Scott little scope for independent action. But the group that opposed Markham underestimated his tenacity. Appealing to the councils of the Royal Society and the Royal Geographical Society, Sir Clements succeeded in having another committee appointed to study the instructions. This body upheld Markham's views, largely because of the superb maneuvering of Sir George Goldie (1846–1925). A retired colonial administrator best known as the colonial founder of Nigeria, Goldie carried the committee with him in endorsing Markham's original plans to subordinate the scientific staff to Scott. The decision turned on the question of where the ship would winter, and in the interests of the safety of the men, Goldie's committee decided that Scott had to have a free hand to take whatever action he thought necessary once he was in Antarctic waters. Scott, not Gregory, would be in control. Gregory thereupon resigned and severed all contact with the *Discovery*. Gregory's supporters argued vehemently that with Gregory's resignation, science would give way to adventure.[13]

Here again Markham had manipulated to secure a naval expedition, his primary goal. With the decision to diminish the role of the civilian scientific staff, the venture became what Markham had wanted all along, a naval voyage of discovery in which science was secondary to adventure. These plans altered British exploration of the Antarctic for an entire generation, lessening the opportunities for research and emphasizing geographical discovery. The voyages of the 1890s had demonstrated the limitations of this approach, but Markham ignored the results of the recent past and sought to recreate what he perceived as the great adventure of Arctic exploration in the 1850s. The victory of Markham's faction ensured survival of the old naval thinking, planning, and practices. One result was the ascendancy of man-hauling, a choice that led to the tragic death of

Scott and his companions in a bitter cold March twelve years hence while returning from the South Pole. They were man-hauling while Amundsen and his companions, moving by dogsled, made the run from their base camp to the pole and back with relative ease. The superiority of dogsled travel over man-hauling was clearly demonstrated during the *Southern Cross* expedition, but Markham overlooked that endeavor and refused to learn from Borchgrevink's experiences.

Similarly, Markham refused to add kayaks as a coastal conveyance. Furthermore, it was foolish, inflated national pride that made the promoters fail to include ski training as preparation for the expedition. Finally, Markham's decision to build the *Discovery*, on the grounds that "no suitable vessel was available," completely disregarded the success achieved by Gerlache, Larsen, Bull, and Borchgrevink using whalers that were readily available at a fourth the cost of the *Discovery*. Compared to existing steam whalers, the *Discovery* was an extravagant monument to the ego of the president of the Royal Geographical Society.

With the major hurdles negotiated, Markham carried other decisions in committee. George Murray (1858–1911), the replacement for Gregory as director of the scientific staff, was in Markham's mind "our man." Scott's authority was left unchallenged. Indeed, Murray journeyed only part way with the *Discovery* and never approached the ice. Markham allowed no rival to challenge Scott or to be in a position to alter the focus of the expedition once it was in Antarctic waters.

In one final issue Markham foisted his opinions on the others. He insisted on a relief ship for the *Discovery*, and the campaign for a second vessel began within sixty days of the expedition's departure. This victory was short-lived, however, and in the end, control of the enterprise was wrested from Markham by a government that had grown weary of his appeals for additional money for a second expedition and his disingenuous attitude about a relief campaign. Markham's behavior in this instance made it far more difficult for future British expeditions to receive prior government funding. For fifteen years no explorer obtained such Treasury support.

At the time of the original deputation to the government Markham had neglected to mention the possible need for a relief expedition, although the idea was clearly in his head. Operating from the fixed tenets of nineteenth-century British Arctic experience, Markham regarded a relief ship as a necessity. As soon as the *Discovery* sailed, he began organizing the effort. He raised money, bought a vessel that he renamed *Morning*, and placed it under the command of Colbeck. During the summer of 1902–3 Colbeck sailed to McMurdo, where he found the *Discovery* trapped in the ice. Supplies were transferred to Scott's ship, and the *Morning* returned to New Zealand. Markham then began campaigning for a *second* relief expedition, this time arguing, in something of a panic, about the need to rescue the ice-bound *Discovery*. When he turned to the government for funds, A. J. Balfour refused. A question in the House of Commons led Balfour to accuse the Royal Society and the Royal Geographical Society of misleading him when they originally sought public funding. Balfour was irate and in the end demanded that the two societies turn the entire effort over to the government, which would then organize a relief effort using the *Morning* and the *Terra Nova*. The council of the RGS took advantage of Markham's absence from the country to agree to Balfour's terms. Markham was livid but could not undo the damage. The expedition that began as Markham's dream ended as his nightmare.

Despite all these shortcomings in the operation of the *Discovery*, credit must be given to Markham for conceiving the idea of an expedition and transforming that dream into reality. The British contribution to the great Antarctic adventures from 1901 to 1904 was made ready. Launched at Dundee on 21 March 1901, the *Discovery* sailed on schedule in August. Amid great ceremony it slipped from its London dock and glided down the Thames as cheering crowds bade farewell. After ten years of planning and scheming, Markham stood on the deck of the *Discovery* as it embarked for the South. He had triumphed over all.

After the *Southern Cross* returned to England in 1900, each man went his own way. William Colbeck returned to the Antarctic in 1902–3 as commander of the *Morning*, sent to relieve Robert Falcon Scott. Louis Bernacchi, who at Cape Adare had written that he hoped never to see such severe conditions again, had a change of heart and joined the *Discovery*. Herlof Klovstad went home to Norway, where, within six months, he died fighting a typhus epidemic.

Carsten E. Borchgrevink returned to Christiania. He visited the United States in 1902 and was sent by the National Geographic Society to Martinique to investigate volcanic conditions. Although in 1909 he announced his intention to lead an assault on the South Pole, the expedition never materialized. He lived an uneasy retirement, distressed that he had never received the recognition he thought he deserved. He became involved in spiritualism; in 1933 Borchgrevink told Mill that he had been in touch with Scott since the latter's death in 1912.

In June 1930 the Royal Geographical Society, celebrating its centennial year, finally awarded its Patron's Medal to Borchgrevink, who thereupon felt vindicated. Old antagonisms were forgotten as Bernacchi and Borchgrevink exchanged cordial greetings in October at Colbeck's funeral, their final meeting. Bernacchi had even written a complimentary note recommending that the RGS bestow the Patron's Medal on his former leader.

Borchgrevink spent his last years in relative obscurity. Once the National Antarctic Expedition had sailed, all interest passed from Borchgrevink to Scott, Markham, and the men of the *Discovery*. Thereafter others—Sir Ernest Shackleton, Roald Amundsen, Richard E. Byrd—occupied the stage of polar exploration. The public remained uninterested in the Norwegian explorer who had helped open the Antarctic before the heroes came.

Notes

Abbreviations

BAASCM
Council Minutes of the British Association for the Advancement of Science, London

DNB
The Dictionary of National Biography, Supplement, January 1901 to December 1911, edited by Sir Sidney Lee (London: Oxford University Press, 1912)

GJ
Geographical Journal

JRGS
Journal of the Royal Geographical Society

PR
Polar Record

PRGS
Proceedings of the Royal Geographical Society

RGS
Archives of the Royal Geographical Society, London

RGSCM
Council Minutes of the Royal Geographical Society, London

RS
Archives of the Royal Society, London

RSCM
Council Minutes of the Royal Society, London

RSE
Archives of the Royal Society (Edinburgh), Edinburgh

RSGS
Archives of the Royal Scottish Geographical Society, Edinburgh

RSGSCM
Council Minutes of the Royal Scottish Geographical Society, Edinburgh

SGM
Scottish Geographical Magazine

SPRI
Archives of the Scott Polar Research Institute, Cambridge, England

Preface

1. Philip W. Quigg, *A Pole Apart: The Emerging Issue of Antarctica* (New York: McGraw-Hill, 1983), 15.

2. It is customary to name Antarctic expeditions before 1922 after the ship that was the primary vessel involved.

3. Louis Bernacchi, *To the South Polar Regions* (London: Hurst & Blackett, 1901), 65.

Chapter 1

1. The first use of the word *Antarctic* in English is credited to Maundev in 1366; Chaucer refers in the *Astrolabe* to "antartik bynethe the Orisonte." *Oxford English Dictionary* (Oxford: Clarendon Press, 1989), s.v. "Antarctic."

2. The five zones were given geographical boundaries, and the frigid zones were believed to extend 24° from each pole. Not all Greek geographers accepted this five-zone theory; Posidonius, for example, rejected the idea of an uninhabitable torrid zone, but his work was generally overlooked. See Preston E. James and Geoffrey J. Martin, *All Possible Worlds: A History of Geographical Ideas* (New York: John Wiley & Sons, 1972, 1981).

3. The most complete account of the ancients and Antarctica is H. R. Mill's *Siege of the South Pole* (New York: Frederick A. Stokes, 1905). Mill's work remains the best single history of Antarctic exploration.

4. Mill, *Siege*, 10–15.

5. Until the South Pole was reached in 1911, various explorers attempted to go further south (toward the South Pole) than any previous explorer. In doing so they established a new record for "furthest south," an awkward term in general use.

6. Mill, *Siege*, 18.

7. I am grateful to Robert Headland of the Scott Polar Research Institute for providing this information from his manuscript on Antarctic expeditions.

8. Mill, *Siege*, 43.

9. Bouvet Island (54° 26' S, 3° 24' E), now controlled by Norway, is about one thousand miles north of the Antarctic mainland.

10. Roland Huntford, *Scott and Amundsen* (New York: G. P. Putnam's Sons, 1980), 6–7; Kent Stowe, *Ocean Science* (New York: John Wiley & Sons, 1985), 16.

11. Cook's chronometer is on display at the National Maritime Museum in London.

12. Paul Recer, "Ice Kingdom," Associated Press Wire Service, 10 October 1988.

13. Mill, *Siege*, 81.

14. James Cook, *Journal*, 21 February 1775, cited in A. Grenfell Price, ed., *The*

Explorations of Captain James Cook in the Pacific as Told by Selections of His Own Journals, 1768–1779 (New York: Heritage, n.d.), 186.

15. For a discussion of early whalers and sealers in this area, see Gordon Greenwood, *Early American Australian Relations* (Melbourne: Melbourne University Press, 1944).

16. Captain Smith reported his sighting of land (62° 40′ S, 60° W) to the British agent at Valparaiso, who dispatched Lieutenant E. Bransfield in the *Williams* to investigate and make any necessary claims. Proceeding south from Smith's discovery, Bransfield discovered Trinity Land (now known as Trinity Peninsula) (64° S, 60° W). Nathaniel Palmer, in the appropriately named sloop *Hero*, was sealing in the area, but his log reveals that he did not observe land until either November 1820 or January 1821. Claims for Admiral Bellingshausen as the discoverer of Antarctica depend in part on discounting the record of Bransfield and Palmer. Soviet accounts such as Martov, *The Geography of Antarctica*, are not the only ones that give credit to Bellingshausen: Ian Cameron, in *To the Ends of the Earth* (London: MacDonald, 1980), accepts Bellingshausen as the formal discoverer of Antarctica.

This controversy has raged throughout this century. H. R. Mill credited Bransfield and dismissed Palmer's claim, while Edwin Swift Balch favored Palmer. An exchange of letters between Balch and Mill took place in *Science* 18 (10 July 1903): 55; 18 (7 August 1903): 182; 18 (4 September 1903): 303. For a detailed study of Bransfield's claim, see Thomas Bone, "Edward Bransfield's Antarctic Voyage, 1819–20, and the Discovery of the Antarctic Continent," *Polar Record* 4 (July 1946): 385–97; and R. T. Gould, "The Charting of the South Shetlands, 1819–1828," *The Mariner's Mirror* 27 (July 1941): 206–42. For support of Bransfield's claim, see also A. R. Hinks, "On Some Misrepresentations of Antarctic History," *GJ* 94 (October 1939): 309–30. For support of Palmer's claim, see W. H. Hobbs, "The Discoveries of Antarctica within the American Sector, as Revealed by Maps and Documents," *Transactions of the American Philosophical Society* 31, pt.1 (January 1939): 1–73; Lawrence Martin, "Antarctica Discovered by a Connecticut Yankee, Captain Nathaniel Brown Palmer," *Geographical Review* 30 (October 1940): 529–52; and J. R. Spears, *Captain Nathaniel Brown Palmer: An Old-time Sailor of the Sea* (New York: Macmillan, 1922).

17. Bellingshausen's account of his voyage is available in English. See Frank Debenham, *The Voyages of Captain Bellingshausen to the Antarctic Seas, 1819–1821* (London: Hakluyt Society, 2d. ser., vol.91, 1945).

18. The first was the Geographical Society of Paris, founded in 1821 by Dumont d'Urville. It was followed by the Berlin Geographical Society (1828), the Royal

Geographical Society (1830), and the British Association for the Advancement of Science (1831).

19. Weddell, an upholsterer's son, went to sea in merchant ships and through self-education became a master. After the Napoleonic wars he turned in 1819 to sealing in the area of the South Shetland Islands. On his second voyage south (1822–24) he established a new furthest south record. His later life is obscure; he probably returned to commanding merchant ships. He died in London in 1834. See James Weddell, *A Voyage towards the South Pole, Performed in the Years 1822–1824, Containing an Examination of the Antarctic Sea* (London: Longman, Rees, Orme, Brown & Green, 1827; rpt. Annapolis: United States Naval Institute, 1970).

20. R. A. Swan, *Australia in the Antarctic* (Melbourne: Melbourne University Press, 1962), 26–27.

21. Huntford sees Parry's voyage as the beginning of the race for the poles. Huntford, *Scott and Amundsen*, 8. Neither magnetic pole is located at the 90° latitude; both constantly drift.

22. The best account of Ross's expedition remains his own record: James Clark Ross, *A Voyage of Discovery and Research in the Southern and Antarctic Regions during the Years 1839–1843*, 2 vols. (London: John Murray, 1847).

23. Sir John Franklin (1786–1847) set out in 1845 in the *Erebus* and the *Terror* to find the Northwest Passage. He and his 128 men perished in one of the major British disasters of the nineteenth century. Relief expeditions were sent out to no avail. Franklin became a Victorian idol, and the legend of his struggles was widely known to British subjects in the second half of the nineteenth century. Typically, Huntford is harshly critical of Franklin and his methods, describing the explorer as a "pathetic, well-meaning blunderer." See Huntford, *Scott and Amundsen*, 10–11. An interesting recent work that uses modern forensic methods to determine the fate of the Franklin expedition through examination of the graves of Franklin's men is Owen Beattie and John Geiger, *Frozen in Time: Unlocking the Secrets of the Franklin Expedition* (New York: E. P. Dutton, 1987).

24. Cameron, *Ends of the Earth*, 132.

25. Swan, *Australia in the Antarctic*, 32–33; Stowe, *Ocean Science*, 18. Maury, a Virginian, left his post in the federal government to fight with the Confederacy.

26. Swan, *Australia in the Antarctic*, 34–35. Work in Germany was continued by the German Society for Polar Navigation in Hamburg.

27. For a more detailed account of the *Challenger*, see Eric Linklater, *The Voyage of the "Challenger"* (London: John Murray, 1972).

28. Borchgrevink spoke about the opportunities for anthropological studies at the International Geographical Congress of 1895, but the academic community gave little credence to the idea of finding Antarctica to be inhabited. On the

Nordenskjöld expedition (1901–3), however, an incident occurred in which separate parties of expedition members came upon each other from a distance and thought each other to be natives—thus demonstrating that Heroic Era explorers had not ruled out the possibility of finding aborigines. See Otto Nordenskjöld, *Antarctica, or Two Years amongst the Ice of the South Pole* (Hamden, Conn.: Archon, 1977).

Chapter 2

1. Swan, *Australia in the Antarctic*, 36. Swan's book is the best account of the efforts of the Australian Committee (see chap.3).

2. Ibid., 40–41. J. N. Tønnessen credits von Mueller's speech with renewing interest in Antarctic exploration. *The History of Modern Whaling* (Berkeley: University of California Press, 1982), 149.

3. Swan, *Australia in the Antarctic*, 51–52, 56–57, 59–60, 77.

4. *The Times*, 20 August 1886, 8; "Geographical Notes," *Nature* 34 (15 July 1886): 247.

5. Captain Crawford Pasco, president of the Joint Committee of the Royal Society of Victoria and the Victorian Branch of the Royal Geographical Society of Australasia, to Admiral Sir Erasmus Ommanney, 22 June 1887, printed in "Geographical Notes," *SGM* 3 (November 1887): 601–4; "Geographical Notes," *Nature* 36 (30 June 1887): 211; "Antarctic Exploration," *Nature* 36 (21 July 1887): 277–78; "Geographical Notes," *PRGS* 9 (September 1887): 576.

6. "The Swedish Antarctic Expedition," *GJ* 18 (October 1901): 448; *The Times*, 13 February 1891, 14; Melbourne *Age*, 21 May 1886.

7. *Spectator*, 8 October 1887, 1339–40; *PRGS* 9 (1887): 444. No account of Nansen's adventures can overstate the greatness of his achievements. Crossing Greenland (1888–89) was his first notable accomplishment as an explorer. He continued with studies of the drift of Arctic polar sea ice using the *Fram*. After his exploring days he was an important figure in achieving Norwegian independence. He represented his homeland in the League of Nations and won the Nobel Peace Prize for his famine-relief work in Russia after World War I. His fame was so great and his name so acclaimed that in the 1920s he issued to stateless persons a document over his own signature which came to be known as the "Nansen Passport." It was accepted by nearly every government in the world. Several biographies exist, but his life and work deserve a thorough treatment. Roland Huntford is currently writing a biography of Nansen.

8. The idea of Nansen's participation in an Antarctic expedition was raised in 1891 with no result. Speakers in Britain attempted to use the possibility of Australian action to spur efforts in their own country. "Notes," *Nature* 44 (9 July 1891): 231; *Spectator*, 8 October 1887, 1339–40; *New York Times*, 23 December 1891, 3;

Swan, *Australia in the Antarctic*, 54–55; "Geographical Notes," *PRGS* 9 (July 1887): 444; *Annual Register* (1891), 129.

9. For a more detailed account of this Arctic work, see Joseph von Payer and Karl Weyprecht, "The Austro-Hungarian Polar Expedition of 1872–1874," *JRGS* 45 (February 1876): 1–19; "International Polar Observations," *Nature* 26 (27 July 1882): 294–97.

10. F.W.G. Baker, "The First International Polar Year," *Polar Record* 21 (September 1982): 277.

11. Ibid. For an account of the life of Wilczek, see Elisabeth Countess Kinsky-Wilczek, *Happy Retrospective: The Reminiscences of Count Wilczek, 1837–1922* (London: G. Bell & Sons, 1934); *Nature* 26 (27 July 1882): 294.

12. F.W.G. Baker, "The International Polar Years: 1882/83, 1932/33, and 1957/59," *Nature and Resources* 18 (July–September 1982): 15–16; G. A. Corby, "The First International Polar Year (1882/83)," *World Meteorological Organization Bulletin* 31 (July 1982): 197–203.

13. For the complete scientific agenda of the first International Polar Year, see *Nature* 26 (27 July 1882): 294–97, which outlines the goals of the program.

14. Baker, "First International Polar Year," 282. William Barr, *The Expeditions of the First International Polar Year, 1882–83* (Calgary: Arctic Institute of North America, 1986), is the most complete account of the first International Polar Year.

15. G. Lecointe, *International Polar Commission, Procès-verbal de la session tenue à Rome en 1913* (Brussels, 1913), cited in Baker, "First International Polar Year," 282.

16. Thomson's specialty was deep-sea flora and fauna. His *Depths of the Sea* (1873) was a landmark book, and his teaching greatly influenced a generation of young naturalists. *DNB*, s.v. "Sir Charles Wyville Thomson."

17. *The Times*, 25 November 1876, 5.

18. *The Times*, 23 November 1880, 6; "Geographical Notes," *Nature* 36 (5 May 1887): 17.

19. "Geographical Notes," *Nature* 25 (16 March 1882): 473; "Notes," *Nature* 26 (17 August 1882): 378; "Notes," *Nature* 27 (4 January 1883): 230; "Notes," *Nature* 25 (27 April 1882), 613.

20. "Proceedings of the Geographical Section of the British Association," *PRGS* 7 (November 1885): 758–59.

21. *The Times*, 18 September 1886, 7; "Geographical Notes," *SGM* 1 (October 1885): 527.

22. *BAASCM* (1885), 1132. Maury postulated that moisture-laden winds were drawn up to great heights within the Antarctic. As they discharged precipitation, heat was given off, with the result that the Antarctic was warmer than the Arctic. See *BAASCM* (1861), 65–72.

23. BAASCM (1886), 278–79; "Notes," *Nature* 36 (25 August 1887): 399.

24. Ommanney to Mill, 11 September 1887, SPRI, 100/89/1; BAASCM (1886), 277–78; Coutts Trotter, "Report to Council," *SGM* 1 (November 1885): 562–63; RSGSCM (6 August 1886), 18; "Geographical Notes," *PRGS* 9 (December 1887): 757.

25. Swan, *Australia in the Antarctic*, 48; "Notes," *Nature* 36 (25 August 1887): 399.

26. "Notes," *Nature* 36 (25 August 1887): 399.

27. *Minute Book of the Royal Society of Edinburgh*, 9 July 1886, 65; 21 July 1886, 1; 23 July 1886, 1.

28. Ettrick W. Creak, "Memorandum on the Advantages from an Expedition to the Region within the Antarctic Circle," *SGM* 2 (October 1886): 619–20; John Murray, "The Exploration of the Antarctic Region," *SGM* 3 (September 1886): 527–48.

29. The Colonial Office to the Secretary of the Treasury, 12 December 1887, reprinted in BAASCM (1888), 317.

30. *The Times*, 7 November 1887, 3.

31. The Lords Commissioners of H.M. Treasury to the Under-Secretary of State, Colonial Office, 3 January 1888, in BAASCM (1888), 317–18.

32. Michael Foster to Colonial Office, November 1887, reprinted in BAASCM (1888), 318–19.

33. BAASCM (1888), 316–19.

34. "Miscellaneous," *SGM* 4 (October 1888): 562; "Notes," *Nature* 38 (5 July 1888): 228; "Geographical Notes," *Nature* 39 (1 November 1888): 19; "Geographical Notes," *PRGS* 10 (November 1888): 712; "Geographical Notes," *PRGS* 11 (March 1889): 177; "Geographical Notes," *Nature* 39 (21 February 1889): 399.

35. H. R. Mill, ed., *Report of the Sixth International Geographical Congress, Held in London, 1895* (London: John Murray, 1896), xiii–xiv.

36. "Geographical Notes," *PRGS* 13 (October 1891): 614.

Chapter 3

1. G. S. Griffiths, "Antarctic Exploration," *Science* 16 (7 November 1890): 257. In times of exceptional scarcity the price could reach ten thousand pounds per ton.

2. Tønnessen, *Modern Whaling*, 753.

3. Nigel Bonner, *Whales* (Poole, Dorset: Blandford, 1980), 145–53; Richard Ellis, *The Book of Whales* (New York: Knopf, 1980), 72–73.

4. Peter G. H. Evans, *The Natural History of Whales and Dolphins* (New York and Oxford: Facts on File, 1987), 255; Tønnessen, *Modern Whaling*, 6.

5. *Antarctica: Great Stories from the Frozen Continent* (New York: Reader's Digest, 1985), 126.

6. For an interesting account of a midcentury American Antarctic whaling voy-

age, see Nathaniel W. Taylor, *Life on a Whaler* (New London, Conn.: New London County Historical Society, 1929).

7. For a list of the American whalers and sealers in this period, see Stuart C. Sherman, *Whaling Logbooks and Journals, 1613–1927* (New York and London: Garland, 1986), 70, 134, 153–54, 344–45.

8. Tønnessen, *Modern Whaling*, 147; *Dundee Advertiser*, 6 September 1892, 6.

9. *Dundee Advertiser*, 31 August 1892, 5.

10. Griffiths, "Antarctic Exploration," 257.

11. *Dundee Advertiser*, 3 June 1893, 3; Tønnessen, *Modern Whaling*, 147–49; Griffiths, "Antarctic Exploration," 257; Frank Bullen, "Antarctic Exploration," *Eclectic Magazine* (October 1897), 564.

12. W. G. Burn Murdoch, *From Edinburgh to the Antarctic* (London: Longmans, Green, 1894), 26; H. R. Mill, "Antarctic Exploration," *Science* 20 (6 September 1892): 202. Murdoch's account is the printed version of the notes he made on the expedition.

13. Details regarding the four ships are as follows:

Ship	Year Built	Gross Tons	Length (ft)	Beam (ft)	Draft (ft)	Engine (hp)
Balaena	1872	417	141	31	16	60
Diana		341	135.5	29	16	40
Active	1852	348	117	28.5	14.5	40
Polar Star		215	125	24	14	

The *Balaena*, originally the *Mjolnar*, and the *Diana* were built in Norway and were purchased as used vessels by their Scottish owners.

14. The cost of the instruments to the RGS was £154 10s. Of the four captains, Robertson of the *Active* was the most diligent in relaying observations to the RGS. For his efforts, he was paid £10. BAASCM (1893), 841; RGS, Expedition Committee Minutes (24 November 1892), 67; "Geographical Notes," *Nature* 46 (15 September 1892): 477; *Dundee Advertiser*, 6 September 1892, 6; Mill, "Antarctic Exploration," 202, 206; Donald to Mill, 20 August 1892, SPRI 100/25/1; Donald to Mill, 8 December 1892, SPRI 100/25/2; RGSCM (28 November 1892), 3; RGSCM (15 January 1894), 3; William S. Bruce, "A Voyage toward the Antarctic Sea, September 1892 to June 1893," *GJ* 2 (November 1893): 430; Bruce, "Cruise of the *Balaena* and the *Active* in the Antarctic Seas, 1892–93," *GJ* 7 (May 1896): 503.

15. *Dundee Advertiser*, 2 September 1892, 6; 6 September 1892, 6.

16. Peter Speak, of the Scott Polar Research Institute, in an interview with the author, November 1988. Speak is writing a biography of Bruce. Currently, the most complete account of Bruce's life is R. N. Rudmose Brown, *A Naturalist at the Poles* (Philadelphia: Lippincott, 1924).

17. *Dundee Advertiser,* 3 September 1892, 3; 6 September 1892, 7; Murdoch, *From Edinburgh to the Antarctic,* 18, 74. H. R. Mill also had a hand in suggesting C. W. Donald. Mill, *Autobiography* (London: Longmans, Green, 1951), 137–38.

18. Murdoch, *From Edinburgh to the Antarctic,* 19.

19. *Dundee Advertiser,* 7 September 1892, 5; 12 September 1892, 5. The *Diana* did put into Madeira en route to the Falklands. H. R. Mill journeyed with the *Balaena* to Broughty Ferry, the first of several Antarctic departures he took part in over the next thirty years. Mill, *Autobiography,* 138.

20. Murdoch, *From Edinburgh to the Antarctic,* 30–31, 132–33, 199–200. The sailors drew half their pay; the other half was paid weekly to family members in Dundee. Ibid., 74.

21. Other popular books were Darwin's *Voyages* and Mill's *Realm of Nature;* Murdoch liked the poet Ossian. Murdoch, *From Edinburgh to the Antarctic,* 110, 118, 143. In later dealings with the Norwegians, Murdoch noted that the men sailing before the mast on the *Jason* appeared to be better educated.

22. Murdoch, *From Edinburgh to the Antarctic,* 48, 87, 119.

23. Ibid., 62–64, 80–82, 130.

24. Ibid., 101–10.

25. Ibid., 165–75.

26. Ibid., 184–85.

27. For a map of the track of the *Balaena,* see Bruce, "Cruise of the *Balaena,*" 509.

28. Murdoch, *From Edinburgh to the Antarctic,* 203, 206.

29. Bruce, "Cruise of the *Balaena,*" 504–5.

30. "The Antarctic Whalers," *GJ* 1 (May 1893): 450; *Dundee Advertiser,* 10 June 1893, 5; Murdoch, *From Edinburgh to the Antarctic,* 232, 239; the quotation is from Murdoch, 272.

31. C. W. Donald, "The Late Expedition to the Antarctic," *SGM* 10 (February 1894): 63; Bruce, "Voyage toward the Antarctic Sea," 436; Murdoch, *From Edinburgh to the Antarctic,* 243–44.

32. Bruce, "Voyage toward the Antarctic Sea," 430–31; Bruce, "Cruise of the *Balaena,*" 507; Murdoch, *From Edinburgh to the Antarctic,* 287, 291. For the view that whales were missed by the Dundee whalers, see the comments of the chief officer of the *Diana* in the *Dundee Advertiser,* 21 June 1893, 5, or the reactions of Captain Robertson, *Dundee Advertiser,* 10 June 1893, 5.

33. Markham wrote at the time of the Scottish whaling expedition that Ross had mentioned in his narrative black whales but never right whales. See Clements R. Markham, "The Need for an Antarctic Expedition," *Nineteenth Century* 38 (October 1895): 706.

34. The *Polar Star* first reported the expedition, on returning to Port Stanley on

17 February 1893. Altogether the four ships took more than sixteen thousand seals during the voyage. *Dundee Advertiser,* 15 April 1893, 5.

35. The *Jason,* powered by a 60-horsepower engine, was 147 feet long and had a 30-foot beam and a draft of 17 feet. It was 495 gross tons and was built in 1881.

36. John Murray, "The Renewal of Antarctic Exploration," *GJ* 3 (January 1894): 36; Tønnessen, *Modern Whaling,* 150–51. Such unlikely reunions also occurred when Nathaniel Palmer and Admiral G. Bellingshausen met in 1821 (see Chapter One) and when Robert Falcon Scott's *Discovery* encountered Roald Amundsen's *Fram* in 1911 as both expeditions were preparing for a dash to the South Pole.

37. John Murray, "Notes on an Important Geographical Discovery in the Antarctic Regions," *SGM* 10 (April 1894): 195–99; "Geographical Notes," *SGM* 11 (April 1895): 201; and C. A. Larsen, "The Voyage of the *Jason* to the Antarctic Regions," *GJ* 4 (October 1894): 336–37. Fossils found on Cape Seymour included pieces of a coniferous tree.

38. Larsen, "Voyage of the *Jason*," 333–34. This comment was referred to by those who, in the 1890s, still hoped for the discovery of a lost tribe of Antarctic natives. See F. A. Cook, "The Possibilities of Human Life within the Antarctic," *Independent,* 24 May 1900, 1245–48.

39. RGSCM (13 May 1895), 3; "Notes," *Nature* 49 (12 April 1894): 559; Murray, "Important Geographical Discovery"; Larsen, "Voyage of the *Jason*," 333–44. After its Antarctic sailing days the *Jason* was sold and renamed *Stella Polare;* it took the duke of Abruzzi to Franz Josef Land and established a new furthest north. Mill, *Siege,* 379.

40. *Saturday Review* 82 (5 September 1896): 265.

41. H. J. Bull, *The Cruise of the "Antarctic" to the South Polar Regions* (London: Edward Arnold, 1896), 8–18; Borchgrevink, "First Landing on the Antarctic Continent," *Century* 51 (January 1896): 433.

42. Bull, *Cruise of the "Antarctic,"* 18–24; quotation is from 18–19. Just before the *Antarctic* sailed, Foyn inspected the ship and insisted on going into the boiler to examine it himself.

43. Bull, *Cruise of the "Antarctic,"* 29.

44. Ibid., 91.

45. Ibid., 57–58. For similar suggestions about international control of whaling and sealing in the Antarctic, see ibid., 225–28.

46. Ibid., 94, 98–100, 102; quotations are from 94 and 103.

47. Ibid., 105–6.

48. R. A. Swan, "A Nineteenth Century 'New Australian' in the Antarctic," *Royal Australian Historical Society, Journal and Proceedings* 46 (1960): 5–8. Burn Mur-

doch had considered this ploy before the position of assistant surgeon was available.

49. Bull, *Cruise of the "Antarctic,"* 121, 126.

50. C. E. Borchgrevink, "The *Antarctic*'s Voyage to the Antarctic," *GJ* 5 (June 1895): 585–87; "Geographical Notes," *SGM* 11 (July 1895): 372–73; C. E. Borchgrevink, "The Voyage of the *Antarctic* to Victoria Land," *Nature* 52 (15 August 1895): 376.

51. *GJ* 5 (June 1895): 587–88; Donald, "Late Expedition to the Antarctic," 65. James Clark Ross named Cape Adare for his friend, Lord Adare. Borchgrevink's lichen is generally accepted as the first discovery of vegetation within the Antarctic region. Sir Joseph Hooker, on the Ross expedition, had found mosses, algae, and lichen on Cockburn Island; before Borchgrevink's voyage, that was the southernmost discovery of vegetation.

52. Of course, this statement ignores the possibility of debarkations by sealers or whalers which went unrecorded. Bruce credits John Briscoe as being the first man to touch shore within the Antarctic Circle, at Adelaide Island, in 1831. Bruce, "The Story of the Antarctic," *SGM* 10 (February 1894): 59. Edouard A. Stackpole claims that Captain John Davis, an American whaler, made the first landing on 7 February 1821, but the evidence is inconclusive. Davis put ashore, but there is no indication that he did so on the continent rather than on an island off the coast. See Stackpole, *The Voyage of the Huron and the Huntress* (Mystic, Conn.: Marine Historical Association, 1955), 51.

53. Bull, *Cruise of the "Antarctic,"* 180–81; Borchgrevink, "First Landing," 440–41. For Borchgrevink's rather modest view immediately after the return of the *Antarctic*, see the summary of his remarks before the Royal Geographical Society of Australasia, 19 March 1895, reprinted in *GJ* 5 (June 1895): 589; compare his comments by 1896 in which he boldly asserted his claim as the first man on the continent when interviewed by the *New York Times* (25 March 1896, 5).

54. Bull, *Cruise of the "Antarctic,"* 180–85.

55. Ibid., 181.

56. *GJ* 5 (June 1895): 589; Bull, *Cruise of the "Antarctic,"* 181, 198, 208–10; quotations are from Bull, 206, 209.

57. *GJ* 5 (June 1895): 588; Bull, *Cruise of the "Antarctic,"* 211–13.

58. Mill, "Antarctic Exploration," 202.

59. Donald to Mill, 8 December 1892, SPRI 100/25/2; "The Antarctic Whalers," *GJ* 1 (April 1893): 362; Bruce, "Voyage toward the Antarctic Sea," 430–31; Bruce, "Cruise of the *Balaena*," 508; *The Times*, 27 May 1893, 5; quotation is from Bruce, "Voyage toward the Antarctic Sea," 431.

60. BAASCM (1893), 807–8; Bruce in Murdoch, *From Edinburgh to the Antarctic,* 359–61. In the late 1980s the largest Antarctic iceberg ever sighted was observed in the Ross Sea. It measured ninety-five miles long and twenty-two miles wide, roughly the size of Hong Kong. Associated Press Wire Service, 15 March 1989.

61. BAASCM (1893), 807–8; "Polar Regions," *GJ* 2 (July 1893): 69; Donald, "Late Expedition to the Antarctic," 67; quotation is from Bruce, "Voyage toward the Antarctic Sea," 431. In all, twenty species of birds were encountered, but the study of the penguin was the most important.

62. For a map of modern whale congregations, see Evans, *Natural History of Whales and Dolphins,* 127.

63. Larsen, "Voyage of the *Jason,*" 337. Arthur Montefiore, "The Jackson-Harmsworth North Pole Expedition: An Account of Its First Winter and of Some Discoveries in Franz Joseph Land," *GJ* 6 (December 1895): 503.

64. "Polar Regions," *GJ* 9 (January 1897): 110; Bullen, "Antarctic Exploration," 571.

65. Murdoch, *From Edinburgh to the Antarctic,* 338.

66. For Bull's view of the reason for the failure of the expeditions to find right whales, see *Cruise of the "Antarctic,"* 217–19.

67. Tønnessen, *Modern Whaling,* 71, 147.

Chapter 4

1. "The Eleventh German Geographical Congress," *GJ* 5 (June 1895): 590; 6:467.

2. In 1908 Cook purported to reach the North Pole, but his claim was discredited by the American geographical establishment, which backed one of its own, Lieutenant Robert Peary. Later, after Cook was jailed for mail fraud, his reputation suffered from his challenged Arctic discoveries and his prison record. Robert Livingston Schuyler and Edward T. James, eds., *Dictionary of American Biography* (New York: Charles Scribners' Sons, 1958), s.v. "Frederick A. Cook." For an apologist's view of Cook, see Hugh Eames, *Winner Lose All: Dr. Cook and the Theft of the North Pole* (Boston: Little, Brown, 1973).

In no way does this controversy play a part in Antarctic affairs in the 1890s except that Cook was attempting to gain fame from Antarctic exploits. At the end of the decade (see Chapter Five) he played a praiseworthy part in the *Belgica* expedition. I have been unable to locate further correspondence between Cook and the National Geographic Society, which has "no record of contact with Dr. Cook before 1909 and his Arctic adventures." Christine Renz, Research Correspondent, National Geographic Society, to the author, 10 March 1989.

3. Throughout the period 1891–1909 Robert Peary attempted to plant the Stars

and Stripes at the North Pole, an accomplishment he claimed in 1909. Cook's announcement of the same achievement had been made only weeks before. Peary had the support of influential geographers, financiers, and politicians, and his claim prevailed despite glaring inconsistencies and questionable record keeping. Dennis Rawlins, *Peary at the North Pole: Fact or Fiction* (Washington and New York: Robert B. Luce, 1973), made a convincing case that Peary had lied. Those societies involved in the case years earlier were less than enthusiastic about Rawlins's work. Rawlins published his book without definitive evidence proving his case, but fifteen years later a chance reference led him to a note in the Peary archives wherein Peary essentially admitted that he had lied. Boyce Rensberger, "Peary's Notes Show He Faked Claim," Associated Press Wire Service, 12 October 1988. Most recently, Wally Herbert has argued that Peary miscalculated and then decided to lie about reaching the North Pole. Herbert, *The Noose of Laurels: The Discovery of the North Pole* (London: Hodder & Stoughton, 1989). In the spring of 1990 the National Geographic Society reaffirmed its belief that Peary had reached the North Pole in 1909.

On Cook's possible motivation for adventure and the reason for his split with Peary, see Eames, *Winner Lose All*, chap. 1.

4. Cook to the American Geographical Society, 30 December 1893, Archives of the American Geographical Society, New York.

5. For a description of Astrup's adventures with Peary in the Arctic, see Eivind Astrup, *With Peary near the Pole* (London: C. Arthur Pearson, 1898).

6. "An American Antarctic Expedition," *GJ* 3 (January 1894): 63; "Miscellaneous," *SGM* 10 (February 1894): 100; "Miscellaneous," *SGM* 11 (May 1895): 260; "Geographical Notes," *Nature* 49 (21 December 1893): 184.

7. Cook to American Geographical Society, December 1893, Plan for an Antarctic Expedition. On the *Belgica* Cook demonstrated considerable ability as a leader in a difficult situation. Amundsen, later conqueror of the South Pole, said of Cook's character during the cruise: "He, of all the ship's company, was the one man of unfaltering courage, unfailing hope, endless cheerfulness and unwearied kindness." Roald Amundsen, *My Life as an Explorer* (Garden City, N.Y.: Doubleday, Doran, 1928), 28.

8. *New York Times*, 24 April 1897, 1; Gustav Pollak, *Michael Heilprin and His Sons* (New York: Dodd, Mead, 1912).

9. BAASCM (1894), 358–59; "Geography at the British Association, Nottingham Meeting, 1893," *GJ* 2 (October 1893): 330; W. Scott Dalgleish, "Geography at the British Association," *SGM* 10 (September 1894): 473; "Geography at the British Association," *Nature* 48 (5 October 1893): 555; Mill to Bruce, SPRI 101/62/1.

10. Bull to Bruce, 10 February 1896, SPRI 101/27/1; Bull to Bruce, 24 December 1901, SPRI, 101/27/3.

11. *Annual Register*, 1891, 129; Clements R. Markham, "Anniversary Address, 1898," GJ 12 (July 1898): 1; John Murray, "The Renewal of Antarctic Exploration," GJ 3 (January 1894): 25; Jon Sörensen, *The Saga of Fridtjof Nansen* (New York: W. W. Norton, 1932), 191, 193; *New York Times*, 24 April 1897, 1; quotation is from Sörensen, *Saga of Fridtjof Nansen*, 193. The *Fram*, one of the great exploring vessels of all time, had been built to Nansen's specifications by Colin Archer and was used by Nansen on his attempt to drift across the Arctic Sea to the North Pole. It is now preserved in Oslo.

12. *New York Times*, 28 February 1895, 7; "Antarctic Exploration," GJ 5 (May 1895): 488. For a complete account of his voyage, see Nordenskjöld, *Antarctica*.

13. Keltie to Borchgrevink, 15 May 1895; quotation is from Borchgrevink to Royal Geographical Society, 2 April 1895; both in RGS Correspondence.

14. Mill to Bruce, 6 October 1897, SPRI 101/62/1; Bull to Bruce, 10 February 1896, SPRI 101/27/1; *New York Times*, 4 August 1895, 1; 24 January 1896, 13; 29 March 1896, 5; Borchgrevink to Keltie, 20 September 1895, RGS Correspondence; Borchgrevink to Keltie, 25 January 1896, RGS Correspondence.

15. Borchgrevink to Keltie, 19 June 1896, RGS Correspondence; *The Times*, 6 September 1895, 5. Skiing was still relatively unknown outside Scandinavia. In contemporary literature it was often referred to as "Norwegian ski-ing," and comparatively few Britons were proficient in the skill.

16. Borchgrevink to Keltie, 12 April 1896; Borchgrevink to Markham, 19 June 1896; both in RGS Correspondence.

17. Markham to Borchgrevink, June 1896, marked "not sent" in Keltie's handwriting, RGS Correspondence.

18. Borchgrevink to Markham, 24 June 1896; Keltie to Borchgrevink, 24 June 1896; Borchgrevink to Markham, 27 June 1896; all in RGS Correspondence.

19. Markham to Borchgrevink, 1 July 1896; telegram from Borchgrevink to Markham, 2 July 1896; both in RGS Correspondence.

20. Borchgrevink to Markham, 3 July 1896, RGS Correspondence.

21. Borchgrevink to Keltie, 19 July 1896, RGS Correspondence.

22. Borchgrevink to Keltie, 25 August 1896; quotation is from Borchgrevink to Keltie, 20 August 1896; both in RGS Correspondence.

23. Borchgrevink to Markham, 19 June 1896, RGS Correspondence; RGS Expeditions and Instruments Committee Report, 19 June 1896; Borchgrevink to Markham, 13 December 1896, RGS Correspondence; quotation is from RGSCM, 10 November

1896, 3. Borchgrevink's 1896 effort was not mentioned in any published account, including Mill's *Siege of the South Pole*.

24. Kristensen, letter to the editor, *The Times*, 6 September 1895, 5.

25. Clements R. Markham, "The Need for Antarctic Exploration," *Nineteenth Century*, October 1895, 706–12; Borchgrevink to the editor, *The Times*, 9 October 1895, 11.

26. Potter to the editor, *The Times*, 6 January 1896, 11, and 8 January 1896, 13; Borchgrevink to Keltie, 14 January 1896, RGS Correspondence; Borchgrevink to the editor, *The Times*, 11 January 1896, 13.

27. Borchgrevink to Keltie, undated (received 26 September 1896); quotation is from Keltie to Borchgrevink, 26 September 1896; both in RGS Correspondence.

28. Borchgrevink to Keltie, undated (received 26 September 1896); Borchgrevink to Keltie, 6 November 1896; Borchgrevink to Keltie, 25 February 1896; all in RGS Correspondence.

29. H. R. Mill, in *DNB*, s.v. "Sir Clements Markham." Regrettably, there is no full-scale biography of Markham. His cousin, Admiral Albert Markham, published a biography in 1917, but Sir Clements deserves a thorough treatment. Huntford paints an unfavorable picture of Sir Clements in *Scott and Amundsen*, 137–39, 142–43, 146–47.

30. A. Markham, *The Life of Sir Clements Markham* (London: John Murray, 1917); and *Encyclopedia Britannica*, 11th ed., s.v. "Sir Clements Markham."

31. Clements R. Markham, "The Present Standpoint of Geography," *GJ* 2 (December 1893): 483.

32. Murray, "Renewal of Antarctic Exploration," 2.

33. Ibid., 16–17; quotation is from 17. Many were misled by Ross's report of the Great Ice Barrier (Ross Ice Shelf) and thought that this insurmountable ice wall surrounded the entire continent. Currently, scientists believe the ice in parts of the Antarctic is more than 7,500 feet thick.

34. The *Challenger* expedition advanced scientific knowledge enormously: in one deep-sea dredging haul, for example, the trawl brought up 89 different species of animals, of which 72 were new to science. Murray, "Renewal of Antarctic Exploration," 19–21.

35. Ibid., 23–24.

36. Ibid., 24.

37. Ibid., 27–29.

38. Ibid., 29.

39. Ibid., 31.

40. See R. Vesey Hamilton, "On Morrell's Antarctic Voyage in the Year 1823, with Remarks on the Advantages Steam Will Confer on Future Antarctic Explorers," *PRGS* 14 (14 March 1870): 145–52; Murray, "Renewal of Antarctic Exploration," 32.

41. Murray, "Renewal of Antarctic Exploration," 32.

42. Clements R. Markham, "Address to the Royal Geographical Society," *GJ* 4 (July 1894): 21–22; quotation is from Markham memorandum, SPRI 1453/2. Leigh Smith and Murray did not attend the meetings.

43. Report of the Antarctic Committee, 7 December 1893, RGS Committee Book, 145a–d.

44. *DNB*, s.v. "Sir Edward Sabine"; Jack Morrell and Arnold Thackray, *Gentlemen of Science* (Oxford: Clarendon Press, 1981), 353–70; quotation is from 333. Morrell and Thackray have done an excellent job of sorting out the details behind the Ross expedition. Northampton to Minto, 6 January 1839, reprinted in a second volume by Morrell and Thackray, *Gentlemen of Science: Early Correspondence of the British Association for the Advancement of Science* (London: Royal Historical Society, 1984), 298–99.

45. Clive Holland, Introduction to Clements R. Markham, *Antarctic Obsession* (Alburgh, Harleston, Norfolk: Bluntisham Books and the Erskine Press, 1986), xiv.

46. Linklater, *Voyage of the "Challenger,"* 14.

47. Markham, *The R.G.S.: A Personal History of the Society*, 53, RGS 47.

48. RSCM (24 February 1894), 74.

49. RSCM (24 May 1894), 96–101; quotations are from 100.

50. RSCM (22 February 1894), 74–75; RSCM (6 December 1894), 132–34; Foster to Markham, 24 February 1894, RGS MS 1/1/4; RSCM (5 July 1894), 113–14; RGSCM (5 November 1895), 3; RGS, 1/1/5; RSCM (6 December 1894), 132–33; "Geographical Notes," *Nature* 48 (12 October 1893): 574; quotation is from Foster to Markham, 2 November 1894, RGS MS 1/1/5.

51. RGSCM (26 November 1894), 1; Markham to the scientific societies of Great Britain and the Empire, 3 December 1894, RGS 1/2/1. The same letter was sent to a broad range of organizations.

52. Zoological Society of London to the Royal Geographical Society, 17 January 1895, RGS, 1/2/4.

53. Geological Society to Royal Geographical Society, January 1895, RGS 1/2/2; Linnean Society to Royal Geographical Society, 7 February 1895, RGS 1/2/6; Royal Meteorological Society, 23 February 1895, RGS 1/2/7; Liverpool Geographical Society, February 1895, RGS 1/2/11; Meteorological Office to Royal Geographical Society, 24 January 1895, RGS 1/2/5.

54. "The International Geographical Congress," *SGM* 11 (September 1895): 474.

55. "The International Geographical Congress," *GJ* 8 (September 1896): 292.

56. "Geography at the British Association, Ipswich, 1895," *GJ* 6 (November 1895): 461–62.

57. Markham, "Starting the Antarctic Expedition: A Personal Narrative," SPRI 1453/2; RGS Antarctic Committee Report, 5 November 1895, 283–84.

Chapter 5

1. Clements R. Markham, "Anniversary Address," *GJ* 9 (June 1897): 594–95; quotation is from Markham to Goschen, 24 November 1896, RGS Expeditions Committee Minute Book.

2. Neale to Markham, 6 April 1897, reprinted in RGSCM (10 May 1897), 1; RGSCM (10 May 1897), 2; quotation is from RGSCM (10 May 1897), 3, Report of the Expeditions Committee.

3. Markham, "Anniversary Address," 595.

4. Clements R. Markham, "The Need for Antarctic Exploration," *Nineteenth Century*, October 1895, 712.

5. Among those accepting but not attending were G. H. Reid, premier of New South Wales; Sir Hugh Nelson, premier of Queensland; Sir Edward Braddon, premier of Tasmania; and W. T. Reeves, agent-general for New Zealand.

6. RGSCM (31 May 1897), 4; "An Anglo-Australian Antarctic Conference," *GJ* 10 (October 1897): 374–77; quotation is from 376.

7. "Anglo-Australian Antarctic Conference," 381–82.

8. Ibid., 385.

9. "The Monthly Record," *GJ* 12 (July 1898): 75–76; quotation is from Markham to Salisbury, 25 October 1897, RGS Committee Book, Expeditions Committee, 19 October 1897.

10. RGS Expedition Committee Report, 10 June 1898, 60.

11. "The Royal Society's Antarctic Meeting," *GJ* 11 (April 1898): 417–19; "The Royal Society's Antarctic Conference," *Science* 8 (11 March 1898): 343.

12. "Royal Society's Antarctic Meeting," 419–22; "Royal Society's Antarctic Conference," 345.

13. "Royal Society's Antarctic Conference," 343.

14. Ibid., 343–44.

15. Clements R. Markham, "Address to the Royal Geographical Society," *GJ* 16 (July 1900): 10.

16. Georges Lecointe, H. Arctowski, and E. Racovitza, *Expedition antarctique belge* (Brussels: Société Royale Belge de Géographie, 1900), 7, 20; "Proposed Bel-

gian Antarctic Expedition," *GJ* 5 (January 1895): 82; "The Belgian Antarctic Expedition," *GJ* 8 (August 1896): 180; Henryk Arctowski, "The Antarctic Voyage of the *Belgica* during the Years 1897, 1898, and 1899," *GJ* 18 (October 1901): 355; Henryk Arctowski, "Correspondence," *PJ* 19 (March 1902): 388; review of *Through the First Antarctic Night,* by Frederick A. Cook, *Nation,* 15 November 1900, 391.

17. "Belgian Antarctic Expedition," *GJ* 8 (August 1896): 180; "The Belgian Antarctic Expedition," *GJ* 10 (September 1897): 331.

18. "The Belgian Antarctic Expedition," *GJ* 12 (September 1898): 319; Arctowski, "Voyage of the *Belgica,*" 357.

19. Adrien de Gerlache, *Quinze mois dans l'Antarctique* (Brussels: Imprimerie Scientifique, 1902), 36–37.

20. Ibid., 39–40.

21. Frederick A. Cook, *Through the First Antarctic Night* (New York: Doubleday & McClure, 1900), x–xi; Cook, "The New Antarctic Discoveries," *Century* 59 (January 1900): 409–11.

22. Lecointe et al., *Expedition antarctique belge,* 12, 15; Arctowski, "Voyage of the *Belgica,*" 362. This survey corrected many errors in contemporary charts.

23. Arctowski, "Voyage of the *Belgica,*" 376; Lecointe et al., *Expedition antarctique belge,* 36, 39–40.

24. Lecointe et al., *Expedition antarctique belge,* 40.

25. Cook, "New Antarctic Discoveries," 416–18; Arctowski, "Voyage of the *Belgica,*" 381–82.

26. Cook, *Through the First Antarctic Night,* 245; quotation is from 234. Cook had previously published his theory about fresh meat and the prevention of scurvy. See Frederick A. Cook, "Medical Observations among the Esquimaux," *New York Journal of Gynaecology and Obstetrics* 4 (March 1894), 282–86. A recent article explains why Cook's methods were successful. See Charles A. Czeisler, "Bright Light Induction of Strong (Type O) Resetting of the Human Circadian Pacemaker," *Science* 244 (16 June 1989): 328–34.

27. Lecointe et al., *Expedition antarctique belge,* 15; Arctowski, "Voyage of the *Belgica,*" 388–89.

28. "Notes," *Nature* 60 (10 August 1899), 352; quotation is from *Nation,* 15 November 1900, 391. Henryk Arctowski published reports on the scientific results of the expedition; see Arctowski, "The Bathymetrical Condition of the Antarctic Region," *GJ* 14 (July 1899): 77–82, and "The Antarctic Climate," *GJ* 14 (October 1899): 413–26.

29. Kenneth J. Bertrand, *Americans in Antarctica, 1775–1948* (New York: American Geographical Society, 1971), 8.

30. "The Belgian Antarctic Expedition," *GJ* 13 (May 1899): 542–45; "The German Deep-Sea Expedition," *SGM* 15 (March 1899): 143–45.

31. The four quadrants were as follows: Victoria, 90° E to 180°; Ross, 180° to 90° W; Weddell, 90° W to 0°; and Enderby, 0° to 90° E. Sir Clements R. Markham, "The Antarctic Expeditions," in *Verhandlungen des Siebenten Internationalen Geographen Kongress* (Berlin: W. H. Kuhl, 1901), 623–24.

32. Ibid., 626.

33. Ibid., 625.

34. Markham's views of sledging as a manly activity were shared by others. For Charles Beresford's opinion, see John Murray, "The Renewal of Antarctic Exploration," *GJ* 3 (January 1894): 33. On the benefits of dogs, see Huntford, *Scott and Amundsen*, 100, 138, 425–26; Frederick A. Cook, "The Antarctic's Challenge to the Explorer," *Forum*, May 1894, 512.

35. Markham, in *Verhandlungen*, 629.

36. Ibid., 626–27, 630.

37. Balch, letter to the editor, *Nation*, 10 May 1900, 357.

38. BAASCM (1899), 803–4; "The British Association at Dover, 1899," *SGM* 15 (October 1899): 527–28.

39. Clements R. Markham, "The President's Opening Address, 1898–99," *GJ* 13 (January 1899): 8–9; quotation is from 8.

40. James Geikie, "Antarctic Expedition," *SGM* 15 (May 1899): 256; "The Monthly Record," *GJ* 15 (March 1900): 287; quotations are from "The British National Antarctic Expedition," *GJ* 13 (April 1899): 425–26.

41. "The National Antarctic Expedition," *GJ* 13 (May 1899): 529; Clements R. Markham, *The Starting of the Antarctic Expedition*, SPRI 1453/2; Markham to Sir Cuthbert Peek, RGS 2/2/2. The *Discovery*, the lone survivor of the British vessels of the Heroic Era, is now docked at Dundee, Scotland. The craft of the German expedition, specially constructed at the Howaldt Works at Kiel, was a wooden sailing vessel with auxiliary engines capable of propelling the ship at seven knots. Named for the great German scientist, the *Gauss* was, like the *Discovery*, constructed with special attention to the needs of magnetic work. In the German vessel all iron work was coated with zinc, and copper was used as much as possible to reduce interference with magnetic studies. Rigged as a three-masted schooner, the ship was steam-heated throughout and equipped with electric lighting. Since it was felt by von Drygalski and others in the German expedition that the dangers from ice were less than those from the severe storms of the region, the ship was constructed with great attention to seaworthiness. Much less expensive than the *Discovery*, the *Gauss* cost roughly thirty thousand pounds to build. "Geographical Notes," *SGM*

16 (January 1900): 46; Erich von Dryalski, "The German Antarctic Expedition," *Eclectic Magazine* 134 (May 1900): 673.

42. Markham to Sir Cuthbert Peek, 19 April 1899, RGS 2/2/4, Antarctic Expedition Box 1.

43. Parry to Markham, 10 May 1899, RGS MS 2/2/6.

44. Parry to Markham, 7 June 1899, RGS MS 2/2/7.

45. The Joint Committee's letter to the government contained the following statement of estimated costs for the expedition:

Building a suitable vessel	£35,000
Fittings, etc.	4,000
Salaries and wages, three years	20,000
Provisions	8,000
Clothing, outfits	7,000
Coals and stores	10,000
Landing party	6,000
Contingencies	10,000
Total	£100,000

These figures differ somewhat from the original estimate that Markham made in the rough draft of the letter:

Building a suitable ship	£35,000
Fittings, riggings, etc.	2,000
Salaries and wages	18,000
Provisions for three years	5,000
Clothing and outfit	5,000
Stores and coals	6,000
Total	£71,000

RGS, 2/3/5, Markham, draft proposal of costs of National Antarctic Expedition; "The National Antarctic Expedition," GJ 14 (August 1899): 191–92.

46. Parry to Markham, 20 June 1899, RGS MS 2/2/9; quotation is from Parry to Markham, 16 June 1899, RGS MS 2/2/8.

47. "National Antarctic Expedition," GJ 14 (August 1899): 193–94.

48. Ibid., 194.

49. Ibid., 196–97; quotation is from 196.

50. Ibid., 198–99.

51. Ibid., 200.

52. Ibid.

53. Francis Mowat to Lord Lister, President of the Royal Society, 3 July 1899, re-printed in "Government Grant in Aid of Antarctic Exploration," *Nature* 60 (13 July 1899), 256.

54. Harmsworth to Markham, 13 July 1899, RGS MS 2/1/11.

55. Parry to Markham, 3 April 1900, RGS MS 2/2/14; Parry to Markham, 6 April 1900, RGS MS 2/2/15.

56. John Murray, "Address to the Geographical Section of the British Asso-ciation, 1899," SGM 15 (September 1899): 522. The BAAS did add one thousand pounds to the expedition's funds at its general meeting in 1899.

Chapter 6

1. Janet Crawford, "That First Antarctic Winter," SPRI 1367, 40.

2. Hulda Friederich, *The Life of Sir George Newnes* (London: Hodder & Stoughton, 1911), 40–50.

3. Ibid., 51–60.

4. Ibid., 67, 83–85.

5. Ibid., 82, 100.

6. Ibid., 120–25, 136.

7. Clements R. Markham, "The President's Opening Address, November 8, 1897," GJ 10 (December 1897): 567; Markham, "Anniversary Address, 1898," GJ 12 (July 1898): 2; Markham, "Address to the Royal Geographical Society," GJ 16 (July 1900) 10; "Geographical Notes," SGM 13 (December 1897), 663; Eames, *Winner Lose All*, 21.

8. C. E. Borchgrevink, *First on the Antarctic Continent* (London: George Newnes, 1901), 4.

9. The dimensions of the *Southern Cross* were as follows: gross tonnage, 521.7 tons; net tonnage, 276.7 tons; length, 146.5 feet; breadth, 30.7 feet; and draft, 18 feet. Bernacchi, *South Polar Regions*, 332; "The Antarctic Expedition," *Country Life*, 27 August 1898, 229.

10. Borchgrevink, *First*, 13. By comparison, the *Gauss* carried only five scientists.

11. Bernacchi, *South Polar Regions*, 331; quotation is from C. E. Borchgrevink, "First Landing on the Antarctic Continent," *Century* 51 (January 1896): 433.

12. Crawford, "Antarctic Winter," 37–39.

13. Ibid., 58; Borchgrevink, *First*, 17.

14. Borchgrevink, *First*, 16; Crawford, "Antarctic Winter," 57.

15. SPRI 1364; "Correspondence," GJ 19 (March 1902): 387.

16. Henryk Arctowski, "The Antarctic Voyage of the *Belgica* during the Years 1897, 1898, and 1899," *GJ* 18 (October 1901): 383; "Antarctic Exploration," *SGM* 14 (April 1898): 201; "Antarctic Exploration," *Science* 2 (11 October 1895): 480.

17. "The Antarctic Expedition," *Country Life*, 27 August 1898, 229–30; A. Supan, "Antarctic Climate," *SGM* 17 (September 1901): 476; Louis Bernacchi, *Saga of the "Discovery"* (London: Blackie & Son, 1938), 28.

18. Borchgrevink, *First*, 6–7; "Scientific Notes and News," *Science* 3 (10 January 1896): 64; *The Times*, 20 August 1898.

19. Markham, "President's Opening Address, 1898–99," 8; Bernacchi, *Saga of the "Discovery,"* 18, 27; Markham, "President's Opening Address, 1897," 567.

20. Markham to Mill, 28 August 1898, SPRI 100/70/1.

21. Ibid.

22. Ibid.; *The Times*, 20 August 1898.

23. Borchgrevink, *First*, 39–43.

24. Crawford, "Antarctic Winter," 81.

25. Bernacchi, *South Polar Regions*, 8.

26. *PR* 17 (January 1974): 24; *The Mercury*, 3 December 1898, 5.

27. Von Neumayer noted the isolation and self-sufficiency of the explorers, in *The Mercury*, 3 December 1898, 5; Borchgrevink, *First*, 57; quotation is from Bernacchi, *South Polar Regions*, 65.

28. Bernacchi, *South Polar Regions*, 37.

29. Ibid., 38, 54, 58–59.

30. Borchgrevink, *First*, 55–66.

31. Ibid., 66–77.

32. Crawford, "Antarctic Winter," 99–100.

33. Ibid., 126.

34. Bernacchi, *South Polar Regions*, 46.

35. Ibid., 60–61.

36. Borchgrevink, *First*, 84.

37. Ibid., 65–86.

38. C. E. Borchgrevink, "The Voyage of the *Antarctic* to Victoria Land," *Nature* 52 (15 August 1895): 377; "National Antarctic Expedition," *GJ* 14 (August 1899): 197; Borchgrevink, "First Landing," 443.

39. Borchgrevink, *First*, 86.

40. Ibid., 92–94; Bernacchi, *South Polar Regions*, 81–83.

41. Borchgrevink, *First*, 86–89.

42. Ibid., 89–91.

43. Borchgrevink, *First*, 99–100; Bernacchi, *South Polar Regions*, 83–84. Borch-

grevink gives the date of the flag-raising ceremony as 2 March; I have followed Bernacchi's chronology.

44. Borchgrevink, *First*, 100–101; Bernacchi, *South Polar Regions*, 85.

Chapter 7

1. Borchgrevink, *First*, 100–105.

2. Ibid., 103–5.

3. Bernacchi, *South Polar Regions*, 130.

4. Janet Crawford, "That First Antarctic Winter," SPRI 1367, 151.

5. Bernacchi, *South Polar Regions*, 92.

6. Ibid., 93; Borchgrevink, *First*, 106.

7. Bernacchi, *South Polar Regions*, 93–94.

8. Ibid., 90–91. The Adelie penguin, like other fauna at Cape Adare, migrates north. Only the emperor penguin remains on land throughout the winter, the males enduring a bitterly cold and dark period on the ice while incubating the eggs.

9. Bernacchi, *South Polar Regions*, 97; Borchgrevink, *First*, 124.

10. Bernacchi, *South Polar Regions*, 97–106; Borchgrevink, *First*, 116–17.

11. Bernacchi, *South Polar Regions*, 106–7.

12. Ibid., 107–8.

13. Ibid., 109.

14. Ibid., 118.

15. Crawford, "Antarctic Winter," 229; Bernacchi, *South Polar Regions*, 95–96. Plates in the Scott Polar Research Institute testify to the excellent quality produced under difficult conditions. I have been unable to locate the motion pictures.

16. Borchgrevink, *First*, 128, 153.

17. Hugh B. Evans, "The *Southern Cross* Expedition, 1898–1900: A Personal Account," *Polar Record* 17 (January 1974): 24.

18. Crawford, "Antarctic Winter," 227.

19. Ibid., 213–14, 218, 229, 253; Louis Bernacchi, *Journal Kept during the British Antarctic (Southern Cross) Expedition, 1898–1900*, SPRI 353/1/1.

20. Crawford, "Antarctic Winter," 220–21.

21. Ibid., 222.

22. Ibid., 226. "Cheap notoriety" was a phrase used by Bernacchi's mentor, P. Baracchi, chief of the Melbourne Observatory, when the young man announced his desire to go to the Antarctic. The older man criticized such activities as an attempt to seek fame.

23. Crawford, "Antarctic Winter," 224–28.

24. Bernacchi, *Journal*, 2 April 1899; Crawford, "Antarctic Winter," 230–31.

25. Borchgrevink, *First*, 141–50.

26. Ibid., 150–51; Bernacchi, *South Polar Regions*, 139–40. Borchgrevink does not mention Colbeck by name in the description of this incident in his published narrative.

27. Borchgrevink, *First*, 158–62; Crawford, "Antarctic Winter," 239–40.

28. Borchgrevink, *First*, 169–70; E. Ray Lankester, ed., *Report of the Collections of Natural History Made in the Antarctic Regions during the Voyage of the "Southern Cross"* (London: British Museum, 1902), 72–73.

29. Crawford, "Antarctic Winter," 344; Borchgrevink, *First*, 171–74.

30. Borchgrevink, *First*, 180; Crawford, "Antarctic Winter," 242, 261.

31. Crawford, "Antarctic Winter," 245, 260.

32. Bernacchi, *South Polar Regions*, 133; Borchgrevink, *First*, 151.

33. Borchgrevink, *First*, 46, 153.

34. Ibid., 112–15; Bernacchi, *South Polar Regions*, 124.

35. Borchgrevink, *First*, 123; Bernacchi, *South Polar Regions*, 137.

36. Bernacchi, *South Polar Regions*, 134.

37. Ibid., 146, 148; Borchgrevink, *First*, 161.

38. Borchgrevink, *First*, 135; Bernacchi, *South Polar Regions*, 139.

39. Borchgrevink, *First*, 122.

40. Ibid., 135.

41. Ibid., 130–31; *Westminster Gazette*, 17 August 1898; Bernacchi, *South Polar Regions*, 8.

42. Bernacchi, *South Polar Regions*, 138.

43. Bernacchi, *South Polar Regions*, 115.

44. Evans, "*Southern Cross* Expedition," 25; Borchgrevink, *First*, 130–31.

45. Borchgrevink, *First*, 269–70.

46. Ibid., 270.

47. Borchgrevink, *First*, 191.

48. Ibid., 200–8.

49. Ibid., 230–33.

50. Bernacchi, *South Polar Regions*, 195.

51. Ibid., 226.

52. Borchgrevink, *First*, 245; Crawford, "Antarctic Winter," 287–88, 302.

53. Borchgrevink, *First*, 246.

54. In the enforced close quarters of an expedition the crew tend to operate in a low-key emotional state. The arrival of mail from the outside world must have had an electric effect on them. My own experience in Marie Byrd Land with Professor Ian M. Whillans of the Byrd Polar Research Institute corroborated the

stifled emotions that develop in such circumstances. At lunch one day we heard the unexpected sound of an aircraft and rushed outside in time to see it drop a mail pouch. My photo, taken at that instant, shows the eruption of emotion so long suppressed.

55. Crawford, "Antarctic Winter," 309.

56. Bernacchi, *South Polar Regions*, 234–36; Borchgrevink, *First*, 254–58.

57. Borchgrevink, *First*, 259; Bernacchi, *South Polar Regions*, 239–40.

58. Crawford, "Antarctic Winter," 315.

59. Bernacchi, *South Polar Regions*, 256; Borchgrevink, *First*, 268.

60. Bernacchi, *South Polar Regions*, 252; Borchgrevink, *First*, 268.

61. Crawford, "Antarctic Winter," 323.

62. Bernacchi, *South Polar Regions*, 260–61.

63. Ibid., 261–63; Borchgrevink, *First*, 280.

64. Crawford, "Antarctic Winter," 328.

65. Bernacchi, *South Polar Regions*, 269; Borchgrevink, *First*, 279. From this location, considerably closer to the South Pole than Scott's position at McMurdo Bay, Amundsen launched his successful conquest of the pole in 1911.

66. Crawford, "Antarctic Winter," 332–34.

67. Bernacchi, *South Polar Regions*, 277.

68. Borchgrevink, *First*, 293. Borchgrevink (p.292) gives the date of crossing the Antarctic Circle as 28 February.

69. Ibid., 295–96.

70. Crawford, "Antarctic Winter," 346.

71. Bernacchi, *South Polar Regions*, 287–96.

72. For Murray's theory, see his address before the Royal Society in 1898; for Maury's hypothesis, see *The Physical Geography of the Sea* (New York: Harper & Brothers, 1855), 406–18.

73. Bernacchi, *South Polar Regions*, 218.

74. Borchgrevink, *First*, 110, 125; Bernacchi, *South Polar Regions*, 226.

75. Borchgrevink, *First*, 232–33.

76. PR 17 (January 1974): 27.

77. Borchgrevink to the editor, *The Times*, 3 July 1902, 4.

78. Borchgrevink to the editor, *The Times*, 19 July 1902, 6.

79. Lankester to the editor, *The Times*, 26 July 1902, 10.

80. Lankester to the editor, *The Times*, 4 August 1902, 10.

81. Borchgrevink to the editor, *The Times*, 4 August 1902, 10.

82. For linguistic issues, see Crawford, "Antarctic Winter," 214 and 221.

Chapter 8

1. Poulton to the Council of the Royal Society, RS 548; "The Recipients of the Society's Medals," *SGM* 16 (May 1900): 296; "On Research in Geographical Science," *GJ* 18 (October 1901): 409.

2. Von Drygalski was educated at the University of Berlin, subsequently taught at Berlin and Leipzig, and was long an associate of polar enthusiast Ferdinand von Richtofen. Von Drygalski's work in Greenland and India won him great acclaim, and his achievements as a scientist led to his appointment to command the *Gauss*. After the *Gauss* expedition he moved to the University of Munich and participated in the Arctic expedition of Ferdinand, Graf von Zeppelin. In addition to producing an account of his *Gauss* adventures, *Zum Kontinent des Eisigens Sudens* (Berlin, 1904), von Drygalski wrote an important textbook on glaciology, *Gletscherkunde* (Berlin, 1942).

Nordenskjöld's research in Patagonia had made a significant contribution to the study of glacial geology. His scholarly achievements led to his appointment to command the *Antarctic* expedition. C. A. Larsen, who had led the *Jason* on its Antarctic voyages in the early 1890s, was the captain of the ship. For details regarding Nordenskjöld's *Antarctic* expedition, see his *Antarctica*.

3. RGSCM, 18 February 1901, 4; Edward B. Poulton, "The British National Antarctic Expedition," *Science* 13 (7 June 1901), 891.

4. Markham, "The Starting of the Antarctic Expedition," SPRI 1453/2.

5. RGS Committee Minutes, 18 November 1897.

6. Peter Speak, interview with the author, November 1988.

7. Mill to Bruce, 6 October 1897, SPRI 101/62/1; Mill to Bruce, 5 February 1898, SPRI 101/62/2; Mill, *Siege*, 380.

8. Bruce to Markham, 21 March 1900; Bruce to Markham, 15 April 1899; Markham to Bruce, 17 April 1899; all in SPRI 441/16.

9. Mill to Bruce, 5 March 1899, SPRI 101/62/4.

10. Peter Speak, interview with the author, November 1988; Mill to Bruce, 5 March 1899, SPRI 101/62/4.

11. Mill to Bruce, 23 March 1900, SPRI 101/62/6; Markham to Bruce, 23 March 1900, SPRI 441/16.

12. Huntford suggests that Markham may have grown unhappy with his choice of Scott. Huntford also contends that Scott sought the appointment to advance his naval career and manipulated Markham to that end. Huntford, *Scott and Amundsen*, 133–34, 136.

13. Unfortunately, neither of Goldie's biographers discusses his part in the resolution of this problem. John E. Flint, *Sir George Goldie and the Making of Nigeria* (Lon-

don: Oxford University Press, 1960); Dorothy Wellesley [Wellington], *Sir George Goldie, Founder of Nigeria* (New York: Arno Press, 1977). Gregory's resignation created a short-lived outcry from his supporters and those who backed his version of the endeavor. In a lengthy letter printed in the 23 May 1901 issue of *Nature*, Poulton emphasized the fears he and others had that, with Gregory's resignation, science would be subordinated to adventure.

Selected Bibliography

Manuscript Sources

American Geographical Society, New York

British Association for the Advancement of Science, London

National Geographic Society, Washington, D.C.

Royal Geographical Society, London

Royal Scottish Geographical Society, Edinburgh

Royal Society, London

Royal Society of Edinburgh, Edinburgh

Scott Polar Research Institute, Cambridge, England

University of Oslo Library, Oslo, Norway

Newspapers

Dundee Advertiser

Daily Telegraph (London)

Hobart *Mercury* (Tasmania)

Melbourne *Age*

Melbourne *Argus*

New York Times

The Times (London)

Westminster Gazette (London)

Books

Serious students wishing further information will rely on the citations in the notes. More general readers are directed to the excellent bibliography in Roland Huntford, *Scott and Amundsen*, which is especially strong on the period 1901–14. In addition, I list below thirty works dealing with Antarctica from 1890 to 1922 for readers wishing additional information.

Bernacchi, Louis. *To the South Polar Regions.* London: Hurst & Blackett, 1901.

Bertrand, Kenneth J. *Americans in Antarctica, 1775–1948.* New York: American Geographical Society, 1971.

Borchgrevink, C. E. *First on the Antarctic Continent.* London: George Newnes, 1901.

Brown, R. N. Rudmose. *A Naturalist at the Poles.* Philadelphia: J. B. Lippincott, 1924.

Bull, H. J. *The Cruise of the "Antarctic."* London: Edward Arnold, 1896.

Cook, Frederick A. *Through the First Antarctic Night.* New York: Doubleday & McClure, 1900.

Holland, Clive, ed. *Antarctic Obsession.* London: Erskine Press, 1986.

Huntford, Roland. *Scott and Amundsen.* New York: G. P. Putnam's Sons, 1980.

———. *Shackleton.* New York: Fawcett Columbine, 1985.

Kirwan, Lawrence P. *A History of Polar Exploration.* New York: W. W. Norton, 1957.

Linklater, Eric. *The Voyage of the "Challenger."* London: John Murray, 1972.

Markham, Sir Clements. *Lands of Silence.* Cambridge: Cambridge University Press, 1921.

Maxtone-Graham, John. *Safe Return Doubtful: The Heroic Age of Polar Exploration.* New York: Charles Scribner's Sons, 1988.

Mill, Hugh R. *Siege of the South Pole: The Story of Antarctic Exploration.* New York: Frederick A. Stokes, 1905.

Mitterling, Philip I. *America in the Antarctic.* Urbana: University of Illinois Press, 1959.

Nordenskjöld, Otto. *Antarctica, or Two Years amongst the Ice of the South Pole.* Hamden, Conn.: Archon, 1977.

Pound, Reginald. *Scott of the Antarctic.* New York: Coward-McCann, 1966.

Pyne, Stephen J. *The Ice: A Journey to Antarctica.* Iowa City: University of Iowa Press, 1986.

Quigg, Philip W. *A Pole Apart: The Emerging Issue of Antarctica.* New York: McGraw-Hill, 1983.

Reader's Digest. *Antarctica: Great Stories from the Frozen Continent.* New York: Reader's Digest, 1985.

Ross, James Clark. *A Voyage of Discovery and Research in the Southern and Antarctic Regions during the Years 1839–1843.* 2 vols. London: John Murray, 1847.

Scholes, Arthur. *Seventh Continent: Saga of Australasian Exploration in Antarctica, 1895–1950.* London: Allen & Unwin, 1953.

Seaver, George. *Edward Wilson of the Antarctic.* London: John Murray, 1933.

Shackleton, Sir Ernest. *The Heart of the Antarctic.* London: William Heineman, 1914.

———. *South: The Story of Shackleton's Last Expedition, 1914–1917.* London: William Heineman, 1919.

Stanton, William. *The Great United States Exploration Expedition of 1838–1842*. Berkeley: University of California Press, 1975.

Swan, R. A. *Australia in the Antarctic*. Melbourne: Melbourne University Press, 1962.

Weddell, James. *A Voyage towards the South Pole, Performed in the Years 1822–1824, Containing an Examination of the Antarctic Sea*. London: Longman, Rees, Orme, Brown & Green, 1827. Reprint. Annapolis: United States Naval Institute, 1970.

Williams, Frances Leigh. *Matthew Fontaine Maury, Scientist of the Sea*. New Brunswick, N.J.: Rutgers University Press, 1963.

Wilson, Edward. *Diary of the "Terra Nova" Expedition to the Antarctic, 1910–1912*. New York: Humanities Press, 1972.

Worsley, F. A. *Shackleton's Boat Journey*. London: Hodder & Stoughton, 1940.

Index

Ommanney, Admiral Sir E., 18–19,
21–22, 55, 83
Osborn, Sherard, 56, 71
Oscar II Land, 33

Palmer, Nathaniel, 7
Parry, S. Sidney, 73, 76
Parry, William E., 8
Patria: rechristened *Belgica*, 66
Payer, Julius von, 15
Peary, Robert, 43, 79
penguins, 31–32, 41, 68, 103–4
Peterson, Jorgen, 79
Polar Star, 27, 29, 31, 33
Pollux: rechristened *Southern Cross*, 79
Possession Island, 97, 105, 107
Poulton, Edward, 115
Prince of Monaco, 117
Ptolemy, 1, 2
Pythagoras, 1

Racovitza, Emile, 67
Richthofen, Ferdinand von, 72
Robertson, Thomas, 27
Robertson Bay, 87, 97, 103
Ross, James Clark, 8–9, 11, 13, 18–20,
26, 29, 32, 52–54, 65, 69, 104, 107–8
Ross Ice Shelf (Great Ice Barrier), 9, 70,
107, 109
Royal Geographic Society: Antarctic
Committee, 21, 55; and *Antarctic* ex-
pedition, 36; Back Grant awarded to
Larsen, 34; and Borchgrevink, 46–50,
83, 116, 122; and Bruce, 44; Cook's
appeal to, 43; and *Discovery* expedi-
tion, 71, 75–76; and Dundee whaling
expedition, 27; and Murray, 52–55,
64; and Ommanney, 19
Royal Geographical Society of Australasia, 26
Royal Scottish Geographical Society,
19–20, 26, 54
Royal Society, 8, 12, 19, 55–57, 71,

73–74, 114–15
Royal Society of Edinburgh, 19
Rucker, A. W., 74

Sabine, Sir Edward, 55
Savio, Persen, 80, 87, 92–93, 97–98,
100, 108
Scotia expedition, 45
Scott, Robert Falcon, 122; and *Discovery* expedition, 115–16, 119; and
Markham, 120; and South Pole expedition, 2
scurvy, 81
sealing, 6–7, 25, 31, 36
seals: studied by Bruce, 40
Shackleton, Sir Ernest, 28, 108, 113,
122
skis: use of, 81, 85
Southern Cross expedition, 109; Antarctic beauty, 102; at Bay of Whales,
108; Borchgrevink as commander
of, 79, 81–82, 86; at Cape Adare,
86–87, 90–97, 100–101, 103–5, 109,
113; at Cape Tennyson, 107; Colbeck
dismissed, 95; at Franklin Island,
107; "furthest south," 108; Great Ice
Barrier, 107; at Hobart, Tasmania,
83–84, 108; and Jensen, 104; life in
hut, 88–90, 100; penguin eggs, 104; at
Possession Island, 105; scientific work
on, 93–94; ship's departure, 89; ship's
return, 104; staff of, 71, 79, 99; use of
dogs on, 100–102
South Georgia Island, 6, 17
South Magnetic Pole, 12, 46, 54, 57, 70,
81, 109
South Pole, 17
Swan, R. A., 14

Tasman, Abel, 4
Tegethoff, 15
Terra Nova, 121
Terror, 8–9